AND YOU:

THE MODERN MEDICINE

AND YOU:

THE MODERN MEDICINE

Dr. Benjamin Lau M.D.,Ph,D.

Canadian Cataloguing in Publication Data

Lau, Benjamin.
        Garlic and you: the modern medicine

Includes bibliographical references.
ISBN: 1-896817-02-5

        1. Garlic—Theraputic use. I. Title.

RM666.G15L38 1997   615'.32433   C97-900200-1

Apple Publishing Company Ltd.
220 East 59th Avenue
Vancouver, British Columbia
Canada V5X 1X9
Tel (604) 325.2888 • Fax (604) 322.6978

CONTENTS

ACKNOWLEDGEMENTS

When I began garlic research in the early 80s, my colleagues dubbed me with the less-than-complimentary title "Garlic Man." In those days, garlic as a legitimate medicinal agent was looked upon with skepticism. Today, I am still referred to as the "Garlic Man," but the title has shed its dubious connotation.

Since the publication of my first garlic book seven years ago, my office has been bombarded with inquiries on the beneficial effects of garlic from the news media and general public alike. Our work has been featured on CBS News, Paul Harvey News, the New York Times, and many scientific journals, to name a few. Garlic has caught the attention of researchers as well. In the past five years, there has been an average of 50 papers published in scientific journals each year. It is most gratifying to see such interest after our modest beginnings a mere 15 years ago.

In these past 15 years, I have had the privilege of working with a number of graduate students and postdoctoral fellows whose findings are included in this book. I wish to acknowledge the following individuals: Moses Adetumbi, Ph.D., Padma Tadi-Uppala, Ph.D., Lin Li, M.D., Ph.D., Takeshi Yamasaki, D.V.M., M.S., Yongqi Rong, M.D., M.S., Zhaohui Geng, M.D., M.S., Christopher Marsh, M.D., and James Woolley, M.D.

I wish also to acknowledge the financial support for my research from the Chan Shun Research Fund for AIDS and Cancer (Chan Shun International Foundation, Burlingame, California).

Kiok Lim, my capable technician for more than 10 years, retired two years ago. During the time she was in our lab, she assisted me in training 18 postdoctoral fellows, six Ph.D. students and seven master's students. Many of my early studies were meticulously performed by her competent hands for which I again salute her.

My wife, Esther, has been a constant source of encouragement and inspiration. She has answered thousands of inquiries regarding our research either over the phone or in writing. In more recent years, this task has been taken over by two of my capable secretaries: Gwen Tamares and Elsa Frances.

My nephew Brian Liu and his mother Ruth Liu have spent many hours to read and polish up the book manuscript, so has my son Daniel who ironed out many wrinkled spots for which I am most grateful.

Finally, I want to thank my publisher for doing a superb job in making this book available to the public.

CHAPTER 1

INTRODUCTION

Recent studies have shown that the general health of Americans is in jeopardy. While health care costs continue to escalate to a whopping one trillion dollars per year[1], the health of Americans has dipped to an all time low. The United States spends the most money per capita on health care, yet it ranks 17th in the world in life expectancy.[2,3] More prescription drugs are swallowed, more surgeries are performed, and more high technology medical treatments are given than any other time; yet, the risk of people dying has sharply increased.

America faces the same predicament as other developed countries. As countries become more wealthy, diseases of affluence, such as heart attack, stroke, cancer, and diabetes, increase. These diseases are the result of lifestyle shortcomings. Although modern medicine has focused on attempting to control these diseases with drugs and surgery, it has now become a well-known fact that the most cost-effective control of these modern diseases is through prevention.[4,5]

The old adage "an ounce of prevention is worth a pound of cure" still holds true today. A healthful lifestyle incorporating proper diet, exercise, rest, and effective stress management, can contribute to a rich, full life, as well as prevent a host of diseases. Although many factors are involved in developing optimal health, some of which are beyond our control, such as hereditary factors, those which are controllable are the ones we should give attention to. It is important to remember that we can make a difference in how we live.

One very simple food item which is receiving widespread recognition is the lowly garlic bulb. As a result of numerous publications in scientific journals and widespread media attention, I have witnessed a proliferating interest in the efficacy of garlic for health problems by both the scientific community as well as the general public. In fact, one of our early research reports on garlic[6] elicited more than two thousand requests for reprint—truly remarkable when compared to the usual 50 to 100. My first book for the general public, *Garlic for Health*,[7] published in 1988, and later translated into Danish, Dutch, Finnish, Spanish, Swedish, and Chinese, describes studies by my own group of research scientists and graduate students as well as by other international researchers. Since the publication of the first book, interest in garlic has skyrocketed, and my office has been bombarded with calls by the news media and the public at large. Then in 1991, I wrote *Garlic Research Update*,[8] an abridged and updated version for those wanting only a quick glimpse into garlic research. And now because of new findings, I have been persuaded to write a third book, this time with more pertinent information which you should find both interesting and informative.

In this book, I am going to share with you the latest research findings on how garlic may retard or even reverse the aging processes, restore memory loss, boost immune functions, nullify effects of pollution, prevent cancer, reduce stress, overcome allergy, and more... But first, let me share with you how I first became interested in garlic....

CHAPTER 2

THE BEGINNINGS OF OUR GARLIC RESEARCH

My interest in garlic research began 15 years ago when a physician friend mentioned in casual conversation that he was successfully using garlic preparations in his practice for a variety of complaints. I had great respect for this colleague as he was a successful practitioner and had published a great deal of medical literature, so I was baffled as to why a man of his caliber was using folk remedies in this modern age of medicine. In the course of our conversation, he mentioned that garlic is a potent antibiotic and inhibitor of many microorganisms. A physician myself and a professor of microbiology, I began devising in my mind a test to find out if my friend was right.

At the time, my students and I were doing experiments testing the ability of various potent drugs to stop the growth of different bacteria and fungi. Upon returning to my laboratory, I prepared diluted garlic extract, introduced it to several cultures, and stuck them in the incubator overnight. The next day I was astounded to find that the diluted garlic extract did indeed stop the growth of those cultures. In fact, more effectively than some of the potent drugs we were testing at the time.

I shared these findings with one of my Ph.D. students, who immediately went to the library to check out the literature. He found that a number of papers had already been published by microbiologists and other researchers, showing garlic to be a potent, broad-spectrum antibiotic.

We found the interest to be broad and research to be fascinating. There were papers published by Indian, Japanese, and European researchers—as well as some extensive and well-documented studies by American investigators. We discovered that researchers had found garlic to inhibit growth of a variety of microbes, including *Histoplasma capsulatum* (an important fungal pathogen in the central and eastern United States), *Cryptococcus neoformans* (a yeast organism responsible for some serious meningitis), and acid-fast bacteria including species causing tuberculosis.[1-6]

With some persuasion, my student convinced me to guide him on a research project to find out how garlic exerts its antimicrobial property using modern technology available in our laboratory.

STUDY OF INSTANT GARLIC POWDER

This student began his study with 30 pounds of Schilling instant garlic powder (the kind one can purchase in supermarkets) donated to us by McCormick Company. He found that the water extract of this garlic powder inhibits the growth of a variety of microorganisms. His focus was particularly on *Coccidioides immitis*,[7] a mold that causes Valley Fever throughout the western United States, and *Candida albicans*,[8] a yeast organism that has received considerable publicity in recent years. He found that garlic acts on the lipid layer of the membrane, interfering with lipid synthesis *(see Figure 1)* and with the ability of the yeast organism to take up oxygen *(see Figure 2)*. It did not, however, affect the synthesis of protein or nucleic acids *(see Figure 3)*. In other words, garlic causes these microbes to lose their membrane, the lining of their bodies, which results in their inability to breathe. Interestingly, we now know that garlic also inhibits animal cells including human cells from making lipids or fat molecules. Our studies have since been confirmed by other investigators.[9,10]

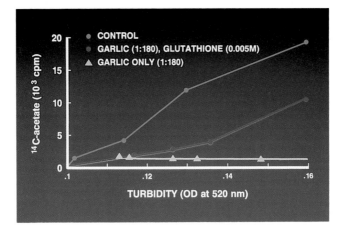

Figure 1. Lipid biosynthesis by *Candida albicans* in the control culture, culture containing garlic, and culture containing garlic pretreated with glutathione. Radioactivity was used to estimate lipid synthesis. The graph shows control without garlic (blue circle) had an increase of lipid synthesis whereas in the presence of garlic (triangle), no lipid synthesis was noted. Glutathione, a sulfhydryl compound, reduced some of the inhibition.

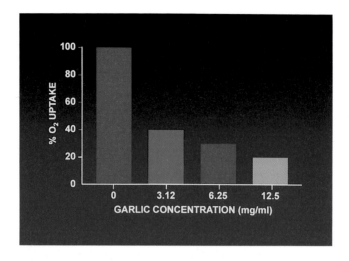

Figure 2. The uptake of oxygen by *Candida albicans* was measured by a Clark oxygen electrode attached to Model 53 Biological Oxygen Monitor and a Curken Model 250 recorder. Inhibition of oxygen uptake is dose-related as shown in the figure.

While most studies, including our own, were done in vitro or in test tubes because of the ease of such experiments, a number of studies have been conducted with animals. For example, researchers in India were able to control *Candida albicans* yeast infection in chicks by feeding them garlic.[11] Studies conducted in Egypt demonstrated the ability of garlic extract to cure ringworm infection in rabbits.[12]

HUMAN STUDIES

What about human studies? Researchers at Hunan Medical College in the People's Republic of China used garlic to successfully treat 11 victims of meningitis caused by *Cryptococcus neoformans*.[13]

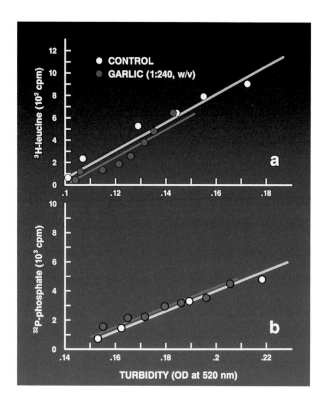

Figure 3. Effect of garlic on protein and nucleic acid biosynthesis in *Candida albicans*. (a) [³H] leucine was used to measure protein synthesis. (b) [³²P] phosphate was used to determine the amount of nucleic acid. The graphs show that garlic extract did not affect the biosynthesis of these macromolecules.

Over a period of several weeks, garlic extract was administered orally and also intramuscularly or intravenously. Side effects were minimal and included transient chills, low grade fever, headache, nausea, vomiting and pain at the site of injection. This type of meningitis was also treated by physicians in Singapore using garlic along with conventional antifungal drugs.[14]

In India, garlic extract applied over the ulcerated tissue was found to clear sporotrichosis,[15] a stubborn fungal infection of the soft tissues and lymphatics usually transmitted from contaminated roses or other thorny plants (that's why we call it Rose Gardener's Disease).

Fungi (yeasts and molds) and viruses cause severe and life-threatening infections in individuals with impaired host resistance. How do the Chinese overcome this problem? Researchers at Beijing Medical University used diallyl trisulfide isolated from garlic as a preventive measure for leukemia patients receiving bone marrow transplants, and found that garlic treatment prevents fungal and viral infections common in these patients.[16]

ANTIVIRAL ACTIVITY

Speaking of viral infections, my colleagues and I are now seeing many patients with chronic fatigue syndrome thought to be associated with such viruses as Epstein-Barr virus, cytomegalovirus, coxsackieviruses, and herpes simplex viruses. Several studies have shown that garlic inhibits viral multiplication. For example, a researcher from the Shanghai Second Medical College, People's Republic of China, collaborating with scientists at the University of New Mexico Medical School reported that garlic has antiviral activity against influenza virus and herpes simplex virus.[17] Two other studies, one from Japan[18] and the other from Romania[19] showed that garlic extract reduces the severity of influenza virus infection in mice. Garlic was also shown to potentiate the antibody response in animals immunized with an influenza vaccine[18] and to inhibit cyto-megaloviruses.[20] Not long ago, a medical student working with me found that human immunodeficiency virus (HIV) or AIDS virus does not grow well in the presence of garlic in tissue culture. The possibilities of garlic are staggering!

Worldwide research continues to show the vast properties of garlic. A colleague of mine doing leprosy research sent me a reprint showing garlic was successfully used in India for treating leprosy.[21] A Tufts University medical student doing summer research at Israel's Weizmann Institute found that garlic stopped the growth of Entamoeba histolytica,[22,23] the parasite that causes nearly 400 million cases of dysentery diarrhea in the world each year. Interestingly, the Tufts University student heard about garlic's curative properties from a Peace Corps volunteer, because no one at Tufts was aware of garlic as a remedy.

Scientists are now interested in finding out which components of garlic exert antimicrobial activity. For years we thought that allicin, the part that gives garlic its pungent odor, was the main component. But, researchers have shown that ajoene is superior to allicin in antifungal activity.[24] Both allicin and ajoene are very unstable. The active ingredient in Chinese garlic preparation is diallyl trisulfide. This compound is quite stable. We have tested this compound in our laboratory and have found it indeed to have a broad-spectrum antimicrobial activity.

Since our publication of the review article "Garlic—a natural antibiotic"[25] more than a decade ago, the number of research investigation confirming the effectiveness of garlic against viruses, bacteria, spirochetes, molds, yeasts, and parasites has proliferated.

In this past decade, many physicians and patients have reported to us that they have fewer colds and also have quicker recovery from viral infections as a result of garlic supplementation. Our own research left us with little doubt that components of garlic indeed have pharmacologic and therapeutic properties against infectious agents. In a later chapter I will share with you our more recent studies with candida yeast organisms.

CHAPTER 3

GARLIC AND BLOOD LIPIDS

While my student concentrated his study on antimicrobial properties, I became interested in the effect of garlic on regulating lipid metabolism. From the literature, I discovered that garlic is used in other countries for preventing as well as treating heart disease. Even though there was a paucity of controlled studies, the idea that garlic may be useful in heart disease is fascinating.

HEART DISEASE:
THE NUMBER ONE KILLER

Heart disease kills about one million Americans a year—almost half as many as all other causes of death combined. Coronary heart disease, the most common type of heart malady, is caused by arteries clogged with fatty deposits and blood clots. When an artery leading to the heart completely blocks the blood supply, a heart attack occurs. If the plugged-up vessel is one that feeds the brain, a stroke results. These fatty deposits are all categorized under a group called lipids, which are insoluble in water.

In 1983, after reviewing world literature regarding garlic and blood lipids, my associates and I published a paper in *Nutrition Research* entitled "*Allium sativum* (garlic) and atherosclerosis—a review".[1] In this paper we reported studies performed by a large number of researchers and physicians showing that garlic can lower blood cholesterol and triglycerides—two kinds of lipids which contribute to atherosclerosis or hardening of arteries. Nearly all the studies conducted up to that time utilized either fresh garlic or raw garlic juice showing this "stinky rose" to be effective in preventing heart attacks and strokes. A few studies indicated that gently cooked garlic was also effective, though somewhat less effective when compared to raw garlic. Two studies using commercially-prepared garlic capsules found no benefit in lowering cholesterol.

In our review of the literature, we noted that in experiments in India and China, test subjects took one ounce or more of garlic every day throughout the study. Would Westerners be willing to do this? Obviously, odor was a stumbling block.

In checking the literature, we found papers by Dr. Asaf A. Qureshi and associates of the US Department of Agriculture.[2,3] In these papers, the researchers evaluated different fractions of garlic extract fed to chickens and reported the odorless water-soluble component of garlic to be just as effective in lowering blood cholesterol and triglycerides as the odorous components. In other words, one need not suffer from the pungent odor in order to benefit from garlic. What good news!

We then discovered from several physicians who were using garlic in their practice that Wakunaga Pharmaceutical Company in Japan had been manufacturing "sociable odorless garlic" for several decades. This pharmaceutical company's research center, with more than 20 Ph.D.s, M.D.s, and D.V.M.s, has been conducting research on garlic and other herbal medicine since 1954. They have published extensively in Japanese journals and in recent years also in American and European journals.

STUDY OF ODOR-MODIFIED GARLIC

In collaboration with two internist colleagues, we decided to conduct a clinical study on blood lipids using the odorless garlic product from Japan; study results were published in *Nutrition Research*.[4]

The first part of the three-part study involved 32 subjects with elevated levels of cholesterol (220–440 mg/dl), randomly divided into two groups. The first group received four capsules a day of Kyolic liquid garlic extract. Members of the other group received four capsules of a placebo—a caramel-colored solution indistinguishable from the garlic extract.

Blood lipids were measured each month. Those who took the placebo showed no significant change. But imagine our dismay when we found that those taking the garlic extract actually experienced an increase in serum cholesterol and triglycerides in the first two months!

We were ready to abandon our research when we found that researchers using fresh garlic had encountered the same results in the first few months. Indian cardiologist Dr. Arun Bordia, studying patients with coronary heart disease, found that garlic supplementation initially raised serum lipids. He postulated that garlic moves lipids from where they have been deposited in the tissues, depositing them instead in the bloodstream.[5] Researchers at the United States Department of Agriculture's Nutrition Institute found the same thing: rats fed garlic extract had fewer lipid deposits in the liver but higher serum lipids.[6]

Buoyed by these findings, we continued our study. Beginning in the third month, we saw a significant drop in serum lipids; by six months, the lipids reached a low level—approaching normal values.

The results? We believe, based on our research, that garlic causes lipid deposits to shift into the bloodstream, causing initially higher serum lipid levels; subsequently, with continued garlic, excess serum lipids are broken down and excreted through the intestinal tract. Several independent studies have reported that this actually occurs in animals who are fed garlic.[7-10]

In the second part of the study, 14 subjects with a normal range of serum lipids were randomly divided into two groups: the first received garlic extract, and the second a placebo. We repeated our method. We were not surprised to find that lipid parameters in both groups remained virtually unchanged by the end of the study. Interestingly, however, among those who took the garlic extract there was a modest rise in cholesterol and triglycerides during the first two months—presumably because garlic mobilized lipid deposits from the tissues to the extracellular fluid.

In the final segment of the three-part study, we again used subjects with high blood cholesterol; they were given garlic extract for six months. After an initial rise in blood cholesterol and triglycerides, 65 percent experienced a drop in serum lipid levels (see Figure 4).

In this part of the study, we differentiated between low-density lipoproteins (LDL), considered to be detrimental to health, and high-density lipoprotein (HDL), known to protect against heart attacks and strokes. Those taking garlic experienced an initial rise in the level of LDL and VLDL (very low-density lipoprotein). The initial rise was followed by a significant drop beginning in the third month. As the study progressed, subjects experienced an increase in HDL (see Figure 5). In other words, garlic can reduce the levels of "bad" cholesterol while increasing the levels of "good" cholesterol.

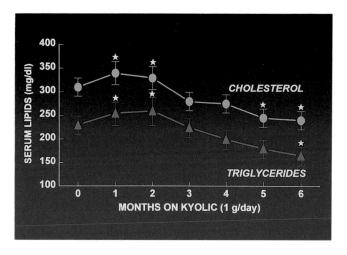

Figure 4. Effect of an odor-modified garlic extract on blood lipids of human subjects. Asterisks indicate significant difference from baseline value. Note initial rise of these lipids followed by significant drop below baseline values while subjects took 4 ml of liquid garlic extract each day.

I mentioned that we were able to observe a significant drop in cholesterol and triglycerides in 65 percent of those taking four capsules a day of garlic extract. What about the other 35 percent who did not respond? Reviewing their dietary history, we discovered that they were heavy meat eaters with diets consisting regularly of steak, pastries, and ice cream, particularly during the evening meals. When we incorporated dietary modification for these individuals, lowering of lipids was then observed in those who followed the recommended dietary changes. Our conclusion is that garlic must be used together with a healthful diet to achieve the best results.

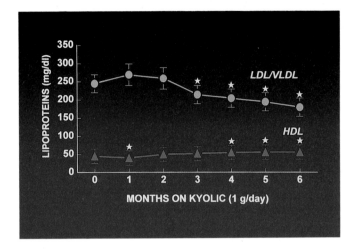

Figure 5. Effect of an odor-modified garlic extract on blood lipoproteins of human subjects. Asterisks indicate significant difference from baseline value. Subjects took 4 ml of liquid garlic extract each day.

The most significant finding of our study was that the lipid regulating effect can be achieved with an odorless commercial garlic product. In the past few years, several companies in the United States and Europe have also begun making odor-modified garlic preparations. These products are available in health food stores and supermarkets. Most of these products have raw garlic enclosed in some type of enteric coating to mask the odor. In addition to studies using the Japanese product, a number of studies using a German product, Kwai, have also shown lowering of blood cholesterol after subjects had taken the product for three to six months.[11,12]

CRITICAL REVIEWS

Recently researchers at New York Medical College analyzed publications dealing with garlic and cholesterol and published their findings in the *Annals of Internal Medicine*.[13] Of the 28 papers they reviewed, five were found to have met the stringent criteria. Our study with Kyolic garlic was one of those five. These authors concluded that controlled studies show garlic can lower blood cholesterol. Another review paper was written by researchers at University of Oxford in England.[14] After analyzing some 30 published papers, including our study, they concluded that garlic therapy over a period of several months is beneficial.

Interest in cholesterol lowering effect of garlic is widespread. People continue to report benefits from taking garlic, not only for lowering cholesterol, but for blood pressure and other risk factors contributing to heart attacks and strokes. But how does garlic help control these risk factors? In the next chapter, I will discuss scientific studies dealing with the way in which garlic affects fat (lipid) metabolism.

CHAPTER 4

HOW GARLIC AFFECTS LIPID METABOLISM

Many of my health conscious patients would like to keep their blood lipid levels low. They are not satisfied with the American "norm" of 200 mg/dl for cholesterol and would like to keep the level below this number. This desire is supported by findings from the famous Framingham Heart Study which show that people with blood cholesterol below 150 mg/dl do not get heart attacks.[1] In fact, death rates from cardiovascular (heart and blood vessels) diseases rise as blood cholesterol goes above 168 mg/dl.[2] Of 10,000 men with cholesterol level of 200 mg/dl, 50 to 60 of them will die of heart attack.[2]

HOW FAT PILES UP

Cholesterol, triglycerides, and other fat molecules in our blood are derived from three sources. The first source is our food intake. The more fatty foods we eat, the more fat will be absorbed into our blood. Whatever our body cannot use will be stored in the tissues and spilled over into the blood. When a person is young and active, much of the fat is burned and very little is stored. When a person is older and not so active however, the fat will be stored in the blood and other places such as the belly to produce a "bay window."

The second source of blood lipids is "endogenous lipogenesis;" in other words, the fats made by our body cells. Nearly all of our cells can make fats, but the main manufacturers are the cells in the liver and the adipose tissues (fat pads). The liver can make fats even from simple sugars we eat in our diet.

The third source of blood lipids is not so much of a source, but is rather associated with a lack of fat breakdown and elimination. Normally our body breaks down fat molecules as a normal process of energy expenditure with the elimination of by-products through excretion. However, if this process does not take place regularly or efficiently, there will be an accumulation of fat molecules in the blood as well as in our body system.

With reference to the second and third sources, I might mention that there are certain culinary items that can augment accumulation of blood lipids by these two means. Alcohol is a prime example. Alcohol has been shown to increase lipids in both the tissues and the blood by enhancing endogenous synthesis of cholesterol and other lipids and by decreasing breakdown of these lipids from dietary intake.[3] Interestingly, when alcohol mixed with garlic oil was fed to rats on a high fat diet, no increase of tissue or blood lipids was observed[3], indicating that garlic reduced endogenous lipogenesis and/or increased lipid breakdown. Having cited this study, let me hasten to add that I do not recommend that people guzzle happily away, basking in the false security of garlic. The long-term deleterious effect of alcohol on our body system is too high a price to pay by any standard.

HOW GARLIC AFFECTS HIGH BLOOD LIPIDS

Getting back to the three main causes of high blood lipids, let's find out now how garlic affects them. The scientific data we have available demonstrate at least three possibilities: 1) Garlic has been shown to either inhibit or reduce endogenous lipogenesis, 2) Garlic has been shown to increase breakdown of lipids and to enhance elimination of the breakdown by-products through the intestinal tract, and 3) Garlic has been shown to move the lipids from the tissue depot to the blood circulation and subsequently to be excreted from the body.

ANIMAL STUDIES

Several animal studies have demonstrated that components of garlic inhibit lipid synthesis by liver cells.[4-7] Feeding rats garlic decreases the activity of several important enzymes involved in the synthesis of lipids not only in the liver but also in other adipose tissues such as fat pads.[8-10] Incidentally, the study by my student using yeast organisms (mentioned in *Chapter 2*) showed that garlic even prevents little yeast organisms from making lipids. So garlic is not only capable of keeping fat off of people, it can even keep microbes like yeast organisms slim, too!

A PHYSICIAN'S EXPERIENCE

Not long ago, a physician friend of mine, after reviewing our paper,[11] decided to put three of his patients with high risk for heart disease on garlic to reduce their blood lipids. These three men had several things in common: They had high cholesterol levels (over 300 mg/dl), each of them was about 50 pounds overweight, they were all truck drivers who smoked and drank a lot of beer, they also had a high fat diet consisting regularly of steak and ice cream, and they practically never exercised.

Anyway, while taking garlic supplement, their blood cholesterol continued to stay up. This doctor was not too concerned in the first three months since he knew from our study that a rise of cholesterol during the first three months of garlic feeding was to be expected. However, at six months their cholesterol levels continued to be high. We discussed the matter and speculated on several possibilities. One obvious possibility was that garlic simply was not working. Another possibility was that these men had such high fat levels in their body tissues that garlic was still moving them out from the tissue to the blood at six months. Thus, when we tested their blood, it continued to be high. Furthermore, because these subjects used alcohol frequently and heavily and had a high fat intake in their diets, they actually fulfilled all three requirements for having high blood lipids. We decided to investigate the second possibility.

Based on data from animal studies, we knew that when there is a decrease of lipids in the organs such as the liver, there may be increased levels of lipids in the blood. So when these men continued to have high levels of lipids in the blood, my natural assumption was that there were less lipids in their livers. Obviously, this was only an assumption since we did not take a liver biopsy to prove it. At any rate, we decided to make some recommendations to these three men. We suggested that they cut down on rich desserts and heavy meals. They all objected to this since they felt that their heavy work deserved heavy meals. We then suggested that they undertake a trial period of no alcohol for one month. Two of them consented. What was amazing was that at the end of the month, their cholesterol levels dropped precipitously! One dropped from 320 mg/dl to 210 mg/dl, a drop of more than 100 mg/dl, while the other dropped from 340 to 280 mg/dl, also a very significant drop. These two cases confirmed our speculations and further demonstrated the effects of alcohol on lipids.

CHANGE OF LIFESTYLE PAYS OFF

One of these men, Gerald, after experiencing this dramatic change in his cholesterol decided on his own to completely give up alcohol and smoking. He also changed his diet and as a result lost the extra pounds. In a recent check-up, he was found to be in perfect health with a much lower risk for coronary artery disease as predicted by the computer printout.

The only thing the computer printout recommended was a regular exercise program. He was receptive to the idea, but like so many of us with hectic lifestyles, Gerald found himself too tired after a long day's work. I suggested that he work exercise into his daily schedule: For example, before hitting the road, Gerald does stretching exercises then walks briskly or jogs for a few minutes. He repeats this process when he stops in a rest area and for meals. All of us can learn from Gerald. Try to work a quick walk or light jog into your lunch breaks. If possible, walk or ride a bike to work. Exercise works wonders for both the body and mind.

Incidentally, I make the same recommendation that I made to Gerald to patients with varicose veins, lower back pain, and sciatica. By stopping every two hours to do light exercise, our bodies and minds become refreshed. For those with varicose vein problems, wearing a light support hose during long trips is also most helpful.

LDL: THE KEY

Before concluding this chapter, I want to comment on the "good" and "bad" cholesterol one more time. The "good" HDL or high-density lipoprotein cholesterol is much denser and heavier than the "bad" LDL or low-density lipoprotein cholesterol. As HDL circulates in the bloodstream, it is not likely to stick to the wall of blood vessels; in fact, it adheres to the low-density lipoprotein, pulling it away from the blood vessel walls and transporting it to the liver, where it is broken down and excreted from the body.[12,13]

Scientists today recognize that the LDL may not be so bad unless it is oxidized by free radicals inside a blood vessel.[14,15] When LDL molecules are oxidized, they are gobbled up by white blood cells in the artery. These white blood cells become engorged and swollen and pack in the artery wall to form plaques. This process eventually leads to thickening and narrowing of the artery. Oxidized LDL's are now considered the very first event that occurs in atherosclerosis. Free radicals may be activated by a variety of factors such as cigarette smoke, air pollution, high fat diets, and even vigorous exercise, to name a few. So the secret to preventing cholesterol clogging and blood vessel thickening and narrowing is to keep LDL's from being oxidized. Studies now show that garlic will do just that.[16-18] We are going to have a whole chapter devoted to antioxidants and free radicals later on. But, now, let's look into some other risk factors for cardiovascular diseases in the next chapter.

CHAPTER 5

OTHER RISK FACTORS FOR CARDIOVASCULAR DISEASES

Myocardial infarction, better known as a heart attack, is the number-one killer in America today; cancer is second, and cerebrovascular disease or stroke is the third. As mentioned in previous chapters, high levels of blood cholesterol and triglycerides are known risk factors for both heart attacks and strokes.

Other blood factors—such as the amount of clotting material and the time it takes for blood to clot—contribute to heart attacks and strokes,[1,2] as do factors like high blood pressure, family history, obesity, cigarette smoking, and diabetes.

HOW DOES GARLIC AFFECT THESE RISK FACTORS?

Blood cells called thrombocytes or platelets normally aggregate or clump together to help prevent blood loss in case of injury; fibrinogen in the blood works with the platelet aggregate through a complicated process to help stop bleeding and to facilitate healing. Without this process, a simple cut could result in fatal blood loss.

A third blood component, plasmin (fibrinolysin), dissolves the fibrin clots when they are no longer needed.

Research has shown that those prone to heart attack and stroke have too much fibrinogen (which causes clots) and not enough fibrinolysin (which breaks up clots). In a book chapter outlining the effect of garlic on these factors,[3] I explained how garlic prevents the formation of clots. In simple summary, garlic prevents the formation of clots, inhibits platelet aggregation, lowers blood pressure, reduces plaque formation in the arteries, and even reverses established arteriosclerosis (thickening and narrowing of arteries).

An epidemiological study of Jain, an Indian community, gives evidence of garlic's impact on the health of the cardiovascular system.[4-6] Those who take garlic as part of their diet have lower cholesterol, triglycerides, and fibrinogen. They also have a longer clotting time, and an increased ability to break up clots when compared to those who do not eat garlic.

GARLIC AND BLOOD PRESSURE

Hypertension or high blood pressure is one of the major risk factors of arteriosclerosis. It is estimated that more than fifteen percent of the adult population in the United States are hypertensive. Few drugs for controlling hypertension are without side effects. One of the most distressful side effects in male patients is impotence. These patients become irritable, frustrated, and depressed.

According to a paper published in *American Pharmacy*,[7] garlic has been used for treating hypertension in China and Japan for centuries and is recognized officially for this purpose by the Japanese Food and Drug administration.

Garlic has been shown to prevent the rise of blood pressure in animal models. As early as 1921, researchers reported the beneficial effects of garlic in controlling hypertension in humans.[8] In the 1940s, one researcher tested 100 hypertensive patients by giving them initially large doses of garlic, then gradually tapering the amount of garlic as the experiment progressed. He reported that after just one week of garlic treatment, 40 of the subjects had a drop of 20 mm Hg or more in their blood pressure.[9] Several small-scale studies have shown similar positive effects of garlic on hypertension.[10-12]

One study in China involved 70 hypertensive patients who were given 50 grams of raw garlic (one average bulb) a day.[13] Thirty-three of the subjects showed a marked lowering of blood pressure; 14 showed moderate reductions in blood pressure, for an overall success rate of 61.7 percent.

A Bulgarian researcher conducted extensive studies involving both animals and humans in an attempt to demonstrate the effects of garlic on high blood pressure.[14-19] This researcher gave cats intravenous injections of fresh garlic juice; at higher doses, the cats experienced only a slight and temporary decrease in blood pressure. But when the garlic had been prepared and stored for seven to 12 months, the blood pressure-lowering activity was significantly increased. Why? It was surmised that storage enabled certain enzyme processes to release active components of garlic. The researcher then tried extracts derived from garlic leaves on 21 humans with high blood pressure. Subjects experienced a systolic pressure drop of 20 to 30 mm Hg and a diastolic pressure drop of 10 to 20 mm Hg. Improvement of other physical symptoms, such as headaches, dizziness, angina-like chest pain, and backaches, was also reported.

Researchers have now demonstrated that garlic is a potent vasodilator,[20,21] acting like some of the drugs currently used for controlling hypertension. Another study found that garlic increases the activity of nitric oxide synthase—the enzyme that increases the level of nitric oxide in our body.[22,23] Nitric oxide (with a chemical symbol NO) is a molecule that is synthesized by the cells lining the blood vessels. Nitric oxide is known to lower blood pressure by relaxing the smooth muscle in the blood vessel. Incidentally, nitric oxide is a very fashionable chemical, so fashionable, in fact, that a few years ago it was named "Molecule of the Year" by the prestigious, highly fashion-conscious journal *Science*.[24] We now know that a decreased level of nitric oxide is one of the hallmarks of atherosclerosis.[25]

A review article recently published in the *Journal of Hypertension* concludes that garlic may be of some clinical use in subjects with mild hypertension.[26] The authors, however, caution the routine use of garlic for treating hypertension and feel that more vigorously-designed, large-scale double-blind studies need to be conducted. The problem is it may not be so easy to conduct such studies. Why? First, garlic is generally classified as an "orphan" drug—one that has therapeutic application but no commercial potential. Without the prospect of financial return, it is not likely that any pharmaceutical company will undertake the task of conducting a controlled, large-scale investigation.

FLUCTUATION OF BLOOD PRESSURE

An additional problem is the fact that blood pressure changes in response to emotional and environmental changes. An Italian hospital study showed how vast these changes can be.[27] In this study, 48 hospitalized patients with high or normal blood pressure had their blood pressure monitored electronically by a recorder that was embedded in an artery for a 24-hour period. During this time, patients were free to move around the hospital except for 30 minutes in the morning and afternoon when routine blood pressures were taken with a manual cuff.

A doctor other than the one assigned to the patients was in charge of taking blood pressures. The systolic blood pressure rose in all but one patient, and the diastolic rose in all but three patients when the doctor came to take blood pressure readings. The systolic rises ranged from 4 to 75 mm Hg, with a mean of 27; the diastolic rises ranged from 1 to 36, with a mean of 15; peak values were reached within one to four minutes of the doctor's arrival. Obviously, human beings are very sensitive to emotional and environmental influences.

SHARING GOOD NEWS OF GARLIC

A common reaction among many of my patients is that they become ardent proponents of garlic and zealously share their experiences with relatives and friends.

One of my patients recommended garlic to his neighbor who had high blood pressure and high cholesterol of above 300 mg. This neighbor was taking medication to control cholesterol but with minimal benefit. Because of the side effects, he began to take garlic in place of his cholesterol lowering medication. When he went back to see his doctor in about three or four months, the doctor was delighted to find his cholesterol had dropped, for the first time in years, to 220 mg. Furthermore, the doctor also noted that his blood pressure was normal. Needless to say the doctor was pleased thinking that the medication was effective!

Shortly after that visit, he quit his blood pressure medicine also. His wife checked his blood pressure every day and found it to be normal. A few months later, this man went back for another check-up, this time his cholesterol had dropped to 170 mg. His doctor was envious of the patient's low cholesterol because his own was 240! Giving credit to the medication, the doctor stated maybe he himself should begin taking it. At this point the man decided to reveal his secret to the doctor. This doctor turned out to be quite open-minded. And in fact, he himself started taking garlic. I saw this doctor's wife a few months ago when she told me of her husband's frightening experience. A month after taking garlic, his cholesterol had risen from 240 to 300 mg! Fortunately, the doctor's wife had read my book and remembered that some of our subjects had initial rise in cholesterol after starting on garlic. She assured her husband that a rise is normal in the first months. At any rate, the doctor's cholesterol is now in the comfortable range of 160 mg. A few weeks ago I saw this doctor at a meeting. He told me he no longer drinks coffee because he has so much energy since taking garlic. He posed a profound question: "How are we going to convince our colleagues it really works?" Jokingly, I told him that's his problem, not mine.

GARLIC AND CHEST PAIN

Last summer, I visited relatives in Illinois. A retired railroad engineer who found out I was there insisted that he speak to me about his personal experience. For 35 years he suffered frequent chest pain from angina. Some doctors thought that his chest pain was caused by heart trouble, possibly compounded by allergy and anxiety attacks. He consulted a number of specialists and was placed on an array of medications—all to no avail. Frequent panic attacks made him wonder if he could make it through another day. While driving on a trip, he listened as his wife read from my garlic book. Ready to try anything, he stopped at a supermarket, purchased a bottle of garlic pills, immediately took two capsules and continued driving. That evening he took two more capsules and continued to do so for the next few days. A week later he suddenly realized that he had been pain-free for the entire week! This happy state has continued for the past five years. A note of caution is in order here: I am not recommending that every one with chest pain rush out to buy garlic pills.

Is it really possible that garlic can eliminate chest pain? I don't have an answer for this question. Although this gentleman insisted that he did not do anything different other than taking garlic, his doctors believed that his chest pain could have been due to blood vessel spasm, or anxiety attack, or some kind of allergy. As a research scientist I want to know why. In terms of the three possible causes speculated by the doctors, I have some explanations. Studies have shown that garlic can relax blood vessels as we mentioned before. We also know that garlic can alleviate anxiety and allergy symptoms which we will discuss in subsequent chapters. Since garlic is not a drug and there is no high profit in it, I am afraid no one is going to conduct research to find out if it indeed can help chest pain.

GARLIC AND DIABETES

Because diabetes is a risk factor in the development of athero-sclerotic disease, it is important to understand the effect of garlic in regulating blood sugar. As early as 1958, Indian researchers found that blood sugar levels dropped when subjects ate garlic.[28] Nearly three decades later, researchers at RNT Medical College in India induced diabetes in rabbits with intravenous injections of alloxan. When fed garlic, the rabbits' elevated blood sugar dropped almost as much as it did when they were given an antidiabetic drug. Researchers postulated that garlic may improve the insulin effect by either increasing the pancreatic secretion of insulin or by releasing bound insulin[29,30] More recently, investigators reported that the sulfur-containing amino acids in garlic controlled diabetes in rats as effectively as the oral diabetic drug and insulin. While diabetic drugs and insulin increased liver cholesterol, garlic did not.[31]

Additional research confirms the effect of garlic on blood sugar. The findings of researchers at the United States Department of Agriculture showed that garlic feeding increased serum insulin levels.[32] Another study by Wakunaga Pharmaceutical investigators showed that aged garlic extract prevented the rise of blood sugar after oral loading of glucose in a standard glucose tolerance test.[33]

AN AMUSING STORY

I can't resist from sharing an amusing story told by one of my patients. Her 82-year-old father had been receiving insulin injections for high blood sugar, but detesting the shots, often refused. A nurse from Home Care came weekly to check his blood sugar. Because it was so high, she warned him of the dangers of not getting the shots. However in recent months, the nurse was pleased that he finally was heeding her warnings, as the blood sugar was now always in the normal range. What the nurse did not know was that the daughter had been giving her father garlic every evening prior to the nurse's visit!

To end this chapter, let me summarize in *Table 1* how well garlic fares with various factors in the cardiovascular system.

It is obvious from the table that the influence of garlic on cardiovascular health is vast. Garlic boosts high-density lipoprotein, increases fibrinolytic activity (needed to dissolve clots), increases blood coagulation time (reducing the risk of clotting disorders), and increases insulin availability. Garlic reduces blood pressure, cholesterol, triglycerides, low density lipoproteins (and their oxidation), plasma fibrinogen, platelet aggregation, and plaque on the arterial walls—for overall benefits to cardiovascular health.

TABLE 1
Effects of garlic on cardiovascular health

GARLIC DECREASES	GARLIC INCREASES
Cholesterol	HDL
Triglycerides	Fibrinolytic activity
LDL/VLDL	Blood coagulation time
Plasma fibrinogen	Insulin availability
Platelet aggregation	Nitric oxide
Elevated blood pressure	
Atheromatous lesions	

CHAPTER 6

PROTECTION FROM ALLERGIES AND ENVIRONMENTAL POLLUTION

Alice and Betty are sisters from Singapore. They came to California for college; Alice majored in science with plans to pursue a career in medicine, and Betty was a music major specializing in piano performance. Both did well during their first year—but during their second year in California, the problems began.

What problems? Both developed the symptoms of allergic rhinitis (hay fever)—runny nose, sneezing, and watery, itchy eyes. Physicians prescribed antihistamines, which somewhat relieved the symptoms but also produced a host of unpleasant side effects, including drowsiness, fatigue, dry mouth, and inability to concentrate. Skin tests indicated multiple allergies, but desensitization shots had minimal effect. It was back to antihistamines, switching from one brand to another in an attempt to reduce side effects. Nothing seemed to work.

Alice's grades suffered; she received several C's and was understandably concerned about getting into medical school. Betty was no better; when she took her antihistamine, her concentration failed, her memory lapsed during performances, and she couldn't practice. If she failed to take the medication, her eyes and nose burned and itched.

Finally their parents wrote to me for help. They had read a paper I had written about the use of acupuncture for allergic rhinitis,[1] and they had also heard about garlic for allergies. They asked for my recommendation, and I gave their daughters a choice.

After one acupuncture treatment, both decided to try garlic (even the most "painless" acupuncture treatment involves some pain). I gave each a bottle of garlic capsules and told each to take six a day.

Within three weeks, both young women were free of hay fever symptoms. Alice finished medical school, and takes garlic capsules now only when the sky is blanketed with heavy smog. Betty graduated with a master's degree in music performance, and teaches in Singapore. Both are free of hay fever symptoms.

There's another interesting highlight to this story. Each year Betty returns to California to visit Alice and other family members. After being free of hay fever symptoms all year in Singapore, as soon as she gets off the plane in Los Angeles she begins to sneeze. A few garlic capsules quickly control the problem. Why does Betty's allergy kick up only on American soil? There must be some reasons.

ALLERGY—AMERICAN WAY OF LIFE

Betty's not the only one. Many who come to the United States to live develop hay fever symptoms after a year or so. Most suffer symptoms all year, with particular sensitivity to smoke fumes, automobile exhaust, smog, and air pollution. A pediatrician who had hay fever and sinus problems for years reports that she has been symptom free since starting to take garlic three years ago. During her yearly visit to Thailand, she used to get flea bites, but not during the last two visits. She attributes this to garlic. In the 1970s, researchers at the University of California in Riverside reported control of mosquitoes, house flies and other bugs with garlic extract in the field work.[2] I know that some gardeners grow garlic around other plants to chase away bugs. Some of my patients have reported rubbing garlic over the exposed part of their body to prevent mosquito bites. But preventing flea bites while taking garlic by mouth is something that I have not heard of before.

GARLIC DETOXIFIES HEAVY METALS

In terms of non-seasonal hay fever we see so much today, the key could be chemicals and heavy metals found in our environment—especially in urban air. Fortunately, studies have shown that garlic can neutralize the toxic effect of various chemicals. A few years ago we performed a simple test to check the effect of garlic on detoxifying heavy metals.[3] *Figure 6* shows ten test tubes each filled with 15 ml of a 5% suspension of human red blood cells. Tube 1 (C) contained 0.5 ml physiological saline and served as a control; Tube 2 (CK) had a 0.5 ml 1:10 dilution of Kyolic garlic extract in saline, and also served as a control. Other tubes—in pairs—contained heavy metals (lead, mercury, copper and aluminum) one in saline and the other in diluted Kyolic garlic extract. As is obvious in Figure 6, heavy metals caused the red blood cells to lyse. Even small quantities of Kyolic prevented the lysis of red blood cells.

Heavy metals are abundant both in nature and in urban environments; lead, for example, is found in automobile exhaust,

paint, and batteries. Mercury, in addition to being found in paint
and batteries, contaminates sea fish and has been used in dental
fillings. If you have a healthy immune system, you can usually
cope with the toxic effect of heavy metals; if not, you can
become ill.

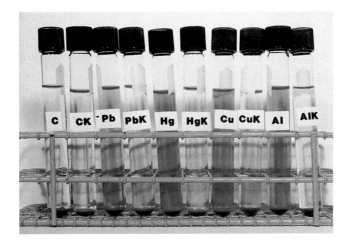

Figure 6. Prevention of lysis of red blood cells by garlic.
C and CK, controls with saline or Kyolic solution,
respectively. Other tubes with metal ions showed lysis
without Kyolic and no lysis with Kyolic in tubes labeled
with K. Pb = lead, Hg = mercury, Cu = copper, Al =
aluminum.

In animal experiments, garlic ingestion was shown to
protect cadmium and mercury poisoning by enhancing
the excretion of these heavy metals from feces and urine.[4]
Many have researched the ability of garlic to aid in
detoxification. In one pilot study, Honolulu dentist Dr.
Samuel Wong used garlic to treat 14 patients with silver-

mercury amalgam dental fillings, and found that garlic facilitated elimination of the mercury from the patients' systems, leading to detoxification.[5]

GARLIC AND LIVER FUNCTION

Detoxification is normally accomplished by the liver—the largest organ in the human body. Besides regulating sugars and metabolizing lipids and proteins, the liver detoxifies alcohol, drugs, and other toxic chemicals that enter the body. When liver cells break down, the liver loses its function—and life is in jeopardy.

Since the liver is such an important organ, I would now like to share with you three studies by Japanese investigators showing the protective properties of garlic against liver cell damage. In one study, researchers, headed by Dr. Tohru Fuwa at the Central Research Laboratories of Wakunaga Pharmaceutical Company in Japan, reported in the *Hiroshima Journal of Medical Sciences*[6] that four of the six sulfur-containing compounds isolated from garlic protected liver cells from damage caused by the toxic chemical carbon tetrachloride. The study was carried out in a rather sophisticated system in which liver cells were maintained in a tissue culture.

This finding was confirmed by Dr. Hiroshi Hikino and associates at the Pharmaceutical Institute of Tohoku University.[7] They found that volatile oil and two sulfur-containing amino acids S-allylmercapto cysteine and S-methylmercapto cysteine extracted from garlic effectively prevented the damage of liver cells induced by two potent liver toxins, carbon tetrachloride and D-galactosamine. Interestingly, they also found that alliin, the precursor of the famous allicin, either did not protect against liver cell damage or did so poorly and certainly much less effectively than the two cysteine compounds. How do components of garlic protect against liver damage? The study indicated that garlic components exerted their protection by inhibiting the generation of free radicals, by preventing the oxidation of lipid peroxides, and thus serving as potent antioxidants. We are going to have a whole chapter later on to discuss garlic as a potent antioxidant.

The third study by Dr. Kyoichi Kagawa's group published in the *Japanese Journal of Pharmacology* looked into the therapeutic rather than the preventive value of garlic on liver damage.[8] In this study, garlic was given to mice by mouth six hours after they had been given carbon tetrachloride. Carbon tetrachloride damages liver cells by a process referred to as "fatty liver." When carbon tetrachloride (CCl_4) is introduced into liver tissue, it is converted to carbon trichloride (CCl_3) which then attacks unsaturated fatty acids in the liver to produce lipid peroxides resulting in the accumulation of triglycerides (fats) in the liver, thus "fatty liver." Dr. Kagawa's study showed that oral feeding of garlic extract even six hours after carbon tetrachloride poisoning was still able to significantly inhibit the formation of fatty liver and thus protect the liver from injury induced by this toxic chemical.

GARLIC NULLIFIES RADIATION EFFECT

Besides pollution, we are concerned about the effects of radiation—so we conducted an experiment to determine whether garlic could provide protection against radiation.[3] We incubated human lymphocytes in tissue cultures for two hours—both with and without Kyolic (2.5 mg/ml) or fresh garlic extract (also 2.5 mg/ml). We also set up tests using L-cysteine (1 mg/ml), a compound known to protect against radioactivity. We then irradiated all but one of each set of cultures with 2000 rads from a Therac-20 Linear Accelerator; each unirradiated culture served as a control (UC).

We tested viability of the cells with trypan blue dye 3, 24, 48, and 72 hours following irradiation. The results are shown in *Figure 7 (p37)*. The unirradiated lymphocytes (UC) remained viable in the tissue culture during the three-day period of observation. Irradiated control (IC) cultures not infused with protective agents steadily declined; within 72 hours, only 25% of the cells were still viable. Cells incubated with L-cysteine or Kyolic (CYS and K) enjoyed significant protection; a few cells died within the initial few minutes, but almost all others were viable at the end of the test period.

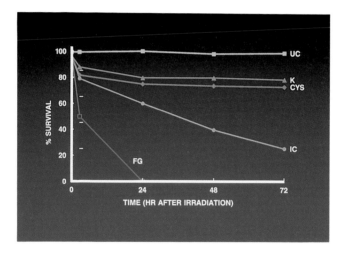

Figure 7. Protection of radiation damage. Unirradiated control (UC) remained viable throughout the experiment. Irradiation of 2000 rads (IC) resulted in death of 75% of lymphocytes at 72 hours. Fresh garlic (FG) caused death of 100% of cells in 24 hours. Protection of radiation damage was observed with Kyolic (K) and L-cysteine (CYS).

FRESH GARLIC TOXIC TO LYMPHOCYTES

Interestingly, the fresh garlic extract (FG) proved extremely toxic to the lymphocytes. Many cells incubated with fresh garlic had died within three hours, and none survived beyond twenty-four hours.

The results of the cultures using fresh garlic raised a number of important questions. Our study showed that fresh garlic extract even in moderate dosage is toxic to lymphocytes. Other studies using fresh or raw garlic have demonstrated other unpleasant effects in addition to the strong odor. Large quantities of raw garlic may cause irritation of the digestive tract. Prolonged feeding of raw garlic to rats causes anemia, weight loss, and failure to grow.[9] For this reason, individuals with existing digestive problems should use cooked garlic or choose a brand such as Kyolic which has removed irritating chemicals yet still retains its pharmacologic principles.

Of the various topics dealing with garlic research, the one receiving the most interest is how garlic can prevent cancer. So in the next chapter, we will consider the potential role of garlic in cancer prevention.

CHAPTER 7

CANCER PREVENTION

Cancer is one of the most dreadful diseases of this modern age. It ranks second only to heart disease as the most frequent cause of death in the United States. What causes cancer? There's no simple answer: many different factors probably lead to the development of cancer. Chemical carcinogens, radiation, and viruses are among those known to us today.[1-3]

Some of the known causes still intrigue researchers, who struggle against time to find a cure. More than two hundred years ago, English surgeon Sir Percival Pott noted a high incidence of scrotal cancer among London's chimney sweepers.[1] He correctly pinned fault on exposure to chimney soot—which we now know contains polycyclic hydrocarbons, known to cause cancer in animals. The chemicals in London's chimney soot are the same class of chemicals that filter into the lungs in cigarette smoke, increasing the risk of lung cancer. Scientists suspect that carcinogens result when some of these chemicals combine with foods and bacteria in the large intestine.

Another well-known cause of cancer is radiation,[2] and much of what we know about radiation's effects comes from studies of people exposed to ionizing radiation. The list includes physicians and dentists who use X-rays for diagnosis or treatment, uranium miners, and nuclear industry personnel, as well as survivors of the nuclear bombings of Hiroshima and Nagasaki. Based on research, we believe that relatively high doses and long periods of exposure are necessary to produce cancer.

Still another cause of cancer—at least in animals—are viruses.[3] Researchers believe that viruses are also involved in some human cancers, including hepatomas (liver cancers) associated with hepatitis B and C viruses, some leukemias associated with retroviruses, lymphomas and nasopharyngeal carcinoma linked with Epstein-Barr virus which causes infectious mononucleosis, and cervical cancer of the uterus linked with papilloma viruses which are also causes of genital warts.

CANCER BIOLOGY AND IMMUNOLOGY

For the past fifteen years, my associates and I have studied cancer biology and immunology.[4-9] Our early research indicated that cancer cells secrete substances that repel cancer-fighting cells, particularly those we call phagocytes.[4,9] As a result, our research has centered on ways to enhance phagocyte activity through various immune stimulants referred to as "biological response modifiers." We've experimented both with live bacterial vaccine and killed bacterial vaccine; both strengthen the body's control against cancer as long as three important conditions are met:

1. The tumor burden has to be low. In other words, the tumor has to be small—either because it has just begun to grow, or because most of it has been removed or destroyed by other means.

2. Dosage and the schedule of vaccine administration are important. Lower dosages generally work better than higher dosages.

The concept "more is better" does not hold true in the use of these biological response modifiers.

3. The route of administration needs to provide optimal contact between the tumor cells and biological response modifier; local routes usually work better than systemic routes (This will be discussed in more detail later).

GARLIC AND CANCER— EPIDEMIOLOGICAL REPORTS

We have also centered our research efforts on the role of nutrition in cancer development and prevention. An epidemiological study reported by the People's Republic of China several years ago[10] intrigued us. Researchers compared two large populations in the Shandong Province. Residents of the province's Cangshan Commune enjoyed the lowest death rate due to stomach cancer (3 per 100,000), but the residents of Qixia Commune had a thirteen-fold higher death rate due to the same cancer (40 per 100,000).

WHAT MAKES THE DIFFERENCE?

The residents of Cangshan regularly eat 20 grams of garlic per day, whereas the residents of Qixia rarely eat garlic. Why did garlic seem to make such a difference? The study showed that Cangshan residents had lower concentrations of nitrites in their gastric juices than those in Qixia who rarely eat garlic. In other words, garlic protects against the formation of nitrites—a precursor of carcinogens—thus providing protection against the development of stomach cancer.

Researchers at the United States National Cancer Institute

collaborated with Chinese scientists and studied 685 patients with stomach cancer and compared them with more than 1,100 matching controls. What did they find? They found that the consumption of garlic and onion was inversely proportional to the risk of developing stomach cancer. In other words, garlic and onion protect against stomach cancer.[11]

Another study on stomach cancer was carried out in Italy. Garlic was found to decrease the risk of developing stomach cancer.[12]

Researchers at Shanghai Cancer Institute reported that salt-preserved meat and fish increase the risk for laryngeal cancer, whereas salt-preserved vegetables do not. The problem was not salt but rather was with the rancid fat in meat and fish. There was a decreased risk for laryngeal cancer associated with green/yellow vegetables and garlic.[13] Another Chinese study, published in the *International Journal of Epidemiology*, reported that green vegetables and garlic have a strong protective effect against colon and rectal cancer.[14]

A large epidemiological project involving more than 41,000 women in the state of Iowa, known as the Iowa Women's Health Study, showed that those who include garlic in their diet have a decreased risk of developing colon cancer. In other words, garlic can prevent colon cancer.[15] The Iowa Women's Health Study also looked into the relationship of fruits and vegetables (including garlic) to development of lung cancer. The results revealed that most fruits and vegetables also have a protective effect against lung cancer in exsmokers as well as nonsmokers.[16] That is good news. However, fruits and vegetables including garlic do not protect against lung cancer in smokers. Two other studies, one involving populations in China[17] and the other in the Netherlands[18] also showed no protective effect of garlic against lung cancer in smokers. The bottom line message from these studies is: to avoid lung cancer, do not smoke; if you are a smoker, quit.

The effect of garlic and diallyl trisulfide (a component of garlic) on the growth of two human stomach cancers was studied by Chinese researchers on tissue cultures. They found that garlic and its component inhibit the growth of cancer cells as effectively as do some chemotherapeutic drugs.[19]

WHAT ARE THE IMPLICATIONS OF THESE STUDIES?

These studies show that garlic may well prevent several carcinogen-induced cancers and that it may also stop the growth of cancer cells. In other words, garlic may show promise for both prevention and treatment.

ANIMAL STUDIES

Many animal studies bear out the same evidence. Studies conducted by Dr. Michael Wargovich in the Gastrointestinal Oncology Section at the University of Texas's M.D. Anderson Hospital showed that organic sulfides, including diallyl sulfide (an important component of garlic), inhibit the development of carcinogen dimethyl hydrazine-induced colon cancer.[20,21] Studies by Dr. Sidney Belman at the New York University Medical Center involving mice showed that topical application of garlic oil prevents skin cancer induced by dimethyl benzanthracene.[22] Researchers at the University of Minnesota at Minneapolis studied mice with benzopyrene-induced stomach cancer. The administration of allyl methyl trisulfide, a constituent of garlic oil, reduced 70 percent of the tumors during the period of the experiment.[23] According to the Minnesota researchers, a component in garlic stimulates an enzyme that protects the stomach from the effects of the carcinogen. Other animal studies show garlic compounds stop the growth of breast cancer, esophageal cancer, and uterine cancer.[24-27]

ANTICARCINOGEN EFFECT

I want to share with you a few of our own studies. We studied several chemical carcinogens, one of which is aflatoxin. Aflatoxin, produced by *Aspergillus* mold, contaminates peanuts, rice, cereal grains, corn, beans, and sweet potatoes, and is linked with liver cancer and possibly with other types of cancer. Liver cancer is one of the most prevalent cancers on the worldwide scale, inflicting large populations in Asia and Africa. Aflatoxin is a procarcinogen meaning it is not a carcinogen in its natural form. It becomes carcinogenic only when it is metabolized or oxidized into the "epoxide" form in our body. In its epoxide form, it can bind to the nucleic acids (DNA or RNA) or protein molecules in the tissue cells and lead to mutation and cancer formation. We now know that there are several ways our bodies can prevent the progression of this process. First of all, our body has ways to inhibit the oxidation of aflatoxin to its epoxide. Secondly, if epoxide is formed, our body can inhibit the epoxide from binding to the DNA. Finally, our body has ways to detoxify the epoxide or carcinogenic chemicals by converting them to water-soluble compounds so that they can be excreted. Glutathione conjugates and glucuronide are examples of water-soluble metabolites that can be excreted from our body.

Figure 8 shows that Kyolic garlic extract and two other garlic compounds inhibit aflatoxin from binding to DNA (top graph). Kyolic also inhibits metabolism (oxidation) of aflatoxin (bottom graph). In addition, Kyolic garlic extract increased the levels of water-soluble glucuronide and glutathione conjugates. We mentioned in the last paragraph in order for aflatoxin to cause cancer, it must first be metabolized to its epoxide. Secondly, it must bind to nucleic acid.

And thirdly, it must cause mutation and cancer formation. Our study showed that garlic extract can inhibit the metabolism of aflatoxin to its epoxide. It can inhibit its binding to DNA. Finally, it can increase the water-soluble metabolites so that the carcinogenic compounds may be detoxified. In other words, our studies demonstrated that garlic can prevent cancer by involving it in all three steps of cancer formation.[28,29]

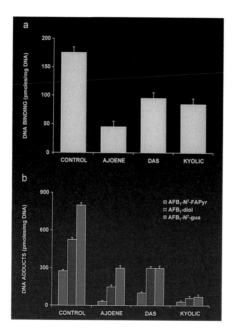

Figure 8. Ajoene, diallyl sulfide and Kyolic inhibited aflatoxin (AFB₁) binding to DNA (Figure 8a). The formation of three AFB₁-DNA adducts was significantly reduced in the presence of these garlic compounds (Figure 8b).

A few years ago, when Dr. Takeshi Yamasaki came to our lab as a postdoctoral research fellow, he brought with him a unique garlic compound called allixin. This is a phytoalexin ("phyto" means plant and "alexin" means to ward off) which is a major weapon used by a plant to fight diseases. Plants do not have a complex defense system like animals, nevertheless they utilize chemical defense to protect themselves. Phytoalexins have been described as "stress compounds" because their synthesis is induced by exposure of a plant to certain kinds of stress, such as contact with bacteria, fungi, viruses, insects, and heavy metal chemicals.[30] Understandably, Dr. Yamasaki wanted to find out if this stress compound plays any role in cancer prevention. He employed all the techniques I described in the last paragraph. Lo and behold, he found that this stress compound allixin prevents mutation (change of DNA), inhibits aflatoxin metabolism and its binding to DNA, and enhances water-soluble byproducts to be excreted, just like everything I reported in the last paragraph with other garlic compounds. We submitted his manuscript to a cancer journal;[31] the editor was so excited about this work, that he accepted this paper for publication in five days! Normally, it takes several months for a paper to get accepted because it usually involves several referees and a lot of time to complete the critique process.

Now I want to share with you a study carried out by Dr. Harunobu Amagase when he was associated with the Pennsylvania State University. In this study, aged garlic extract and a major compound S-allyl cysteine (SAC) were used.[32] *Figure 9* shows that SAC inhibited the binding of chemical carcinogen to DNA of mammary cells of rats.

An interesting finding of this study relates to the food intake and weight gain. The rats used in the experiment were young growing animals. They eat well and grow fast. A is aged garlic powder and B is another commercial garlic product. Animals who took aged garlic (A) enjoyed good appetite, and had normal weight gain. Animals who took the other product (B) had poor appetite and did not gain weight *(see Table 2)*. The point is that not all commercial garlic products are equal.

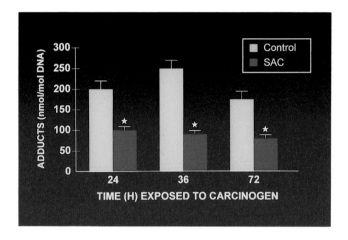

Figure 9. Effect of S-allyl cysteine (SAC) on binding of dimethylbenz[a]anthracene (DMBA carcinogen) to mammary cell DNA. Figure shows that SAC inhibits carcinogen-DNA binding. Adapted from Amagase and Milner with permission.

GARLIC INHIBITS
BLADDER CANCER IN MICE

During this past decade, I have collaborated with several urologists in the study of bladder cancer;[33-35] as mentioned earlier, we have used both live and killed bacterial vaccines and have included garlic extract in our testing. Test results published in the *Journal of Urology*[33,34] show that treatment with a liquid garlic extract, delivered directly into the bladder, produced the lowest incidence of bladder cancer. The same treatment also resulted in smaller tumors.

TABLE 2   Effects of different garlic compounds on food intake and weight gain in rats.

Garlic Diet	Food intake (g per day)	Body weight (g)
Control	11.3	40.8
A 2%	12.2	40.8
B 2%	9.2	19.2
SAC (5 mg/kg)	11.9	44.8
SAC (2.5 mg/kg)	12.4	45.8

From Amagase and Milner with permission.

What happens? Garlic apparently stimulates the body's immune system, specifically by enhancing the macrophages and lymphocytes which destroy cancer cells *(see Figure 10)*.

Our best results occurred when garlic was applied directly to the tumor site *(see Figures 11 and 12)*. Figure 11 shows what happened when animals received only one treatment one day after the tumor was transplanted. Control animals that received only saline had a progressive increase in tumor size. When bacillus Calmette-Guerin (BCG), a live vaccine, was given systemically, the tumor was not reduced, but when BCG was injected locally, the tumor was reduced. However, when either garlic (abbreviated as AS for *Allium sativum,* the scientific name for garlic) or a killed vaccine (*Corynebacterium parvum,* abbreviated as CP) was injected systemically, tumor sizes were reduced—greater reduction occurred when the injection was local.

Figure 12 shows what happened when similar tests were done involving five treatments. As illustrated in the figure, garlic (AS) and the killed vaccine (CP) showed much more effective results than did the live vaccine (BCG), the latter being currently used in the treatment of bladder cancer.

The most remarkable finding about this series of five

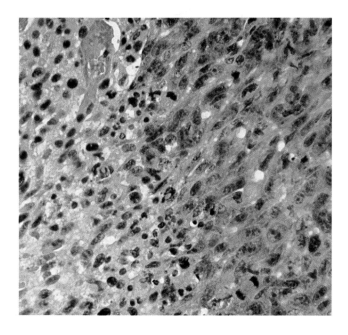

Figure 10. Injection of garlic extract attracts accumulation of lymphocytes and macrophages to the tissue site to destroy tumor.

treatments occurred when we examined the tumors under the microscope. What we had originally thought to be smaller tumors treated by garlic or killed vaccine were actually only scar tissue. There were no tumor cells. In other words, five treatments with these agents actually cured the cancer! Note that the cure was obtained only with local injection, not systemic injection.

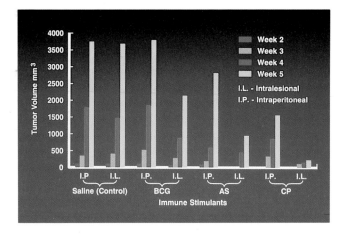

Figure 11. Comparison of intraperitoneal (IP) versus intralesional (IL) immunotherapy one day after tumor transplant.

Nearly forty years ago, researchers at Western Reserve University reported that garlic extract prevented tumor growth by inactivating sulfhydryl compounds of tumor cells.[36,37] Our own studies show that garlic possibly works in a dual role, interfering with tumor cell metabolism on the one hand and stimulating immune cells on the other.

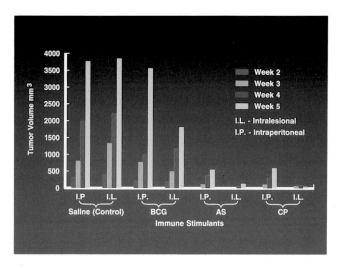

Figure 12. Five treatments of garlic (AS for *Allium sativum*) directly to the tumor site resulted in scar tissue with no tumor remaining.

Several review articles[38-40] including the one written by our group[41] have been published dealing with cancer prevention and tumor inhibition properties of garlic. To conclude this chapter let me summarize the scientific evidence we now have:

Epidemiological studies show that garlic can prevent digestive tract cancers—namely, stomach and colon cancers. In vitro (laboratory) and animal studies show that garlic can inhibit carcinogen formation, and can eliminate or detoxify carcinogenic metabolites. And finally, our own studies as well as those of several other investigators[42-44] suggest that garlic can enhance immune function. This will be discussed in greater detail in the next chapter.

CHAPTER 8

MODULATION OF IMMUNE FUNCTION

The human body consists of several important organ systems, each of which carries on a special function. Of these various systems, the one most extensively studied in recent years is the "immune system." The organs comprising this system are: the thymus, a small organ behind the breastbone; the bone marrow, particularly abundant in the long bones; the spleen, situated in the left side of the belly; and the lymph nodes, scattered in strategic places throughout the body.

THE DEFENSE SYSTEM

Our immune system is very much like the United States Department of Defense. When it functions properly, it protects against foreign invaders and maintains national peace. The Department of Defense employs various branches—the Army, Navy, Air Force, and Marines, to name a few—that help it do its job. Likewise, our immune system employs several major branches—the B lymphocytes (B for bone marrow), the T lymphocytes (cells which are educated in the thymus), the phagocytes (neutrophils, monocytes, and macrophages), and the natural killer cells *(see Figure 13)*. Macrophages are the "national guards" stationed in various parts of our body while other cell types are found in the blood as a part of the white blood cells.

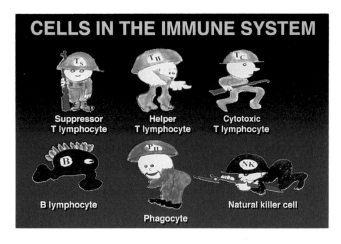

Figure 13. Major branches of military forces in host defense.

FUNCTION OF THE IMMUNE CELLS

The B lymphocytes respond to various stimuli by producing antibodies, which help fight off many common infections. Phagocytes ingest foreign particles and destroy them by using either oxygen radicals or special types of enzymes. The other types of immune cells directly attack foreign invaders, such as cancer cells, bacteria, viruses, or fungi. Some carry out their attack by secreting powerful chemicals called cytokines (cyto=cell, kine=active ingredients). We now recognize at least four subtypes of T lymphocytes: the helper T lymphocytes, which are always ready to help other cells; the cytotoxic T lymphocytes, whose main job is to control foreign invaders; the suppressor T cells, which act as military police to ensure that other cell types do not transgress their limit; and the fourth type of T cell is involved in certain kinds of allergy such as dermatitis in persons allergic to poison oak.

Our paper published in the *Journal of Urology*[1] explained that lymphocytes and macrophages were attracted to the site where garlic was injected. Other researchers have also noticed that garlic attracts immune cells,[2-4] so we decided to do a clear-cut study to see exactly how this is accomplished.

ANIMAL EXPERIMENT

We used three groups of mice in the study.[5] The first group of mice received 0.1 ml of a 1:2 dilution of Kyolic liquid garlic extract injected subcutaneously into the inguinal (groin) area. The second received 0.1 ml of the diluted Kyolic liquid garlic extract injected systemically into the peritoneal cavity (the membrane structure that lines the abdomen). The third group, serving as controls, did not receive any treatment.

Four days after we made the injections, we examined leukocytes from the spleen, the peritoneal cavity, and inguinal lymph nodes. We then use a computerized luminometer to examine the cells to determine how well the leukocytes could engulf and destroy foreign particles. The results are shown in *Figures 14A* and *14B*.

Figure 14A shows the leukocyte response of the mice that received injections of garlic into the groin. Compared to the control mice, those that received the local injections into the groin showed only slightly better leukocyte activity in the peritoneal cavity or spleen—but there was significantly greater leukocyte activity in the inguinal lymph nodes. *Figure 14B* shows the leukocyte response of the mice that received a systemic injection into the peritoneal cavity. Compared to the control mice, those that received systemic injections

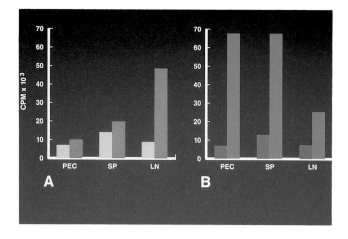

Figure 14. Effect of garlic on phagocyte activity. (A) Mice were given garlic extract subcutaneously into the inguinal site. Compared with controls (yellow bars), only slight increase of phagocyte activity was observed with leukocytes from the peritoneal cavity (PEC) and spleen (SP). Significantly higher activity was obtained with leukocytes from the inguinal lymph nodes (LN). (B) Mice received garlic extract intraperitoneally. Increased activity was noted with all three sites; higher with cells from the peritoneal cavity (PEC) and spleen (SP).

had significantly more leukocyte activity in the peritoneal cavity and spleen—clearly more than in the inguinal lymph nodes. Obviously, if the disease is localized, a localized treatment should be given, whereas systemic disease should be treated with a systemic treatment. In other words, systemic therapy should not always be the automatic choice of treatment.

Similar findings have been confirmed in other studies. One study in Japan showed that certain fractions of garlic extract stimulated macrophages to kill tumor cells and to clear carbon particles from animals' bodies. The same researchers showed that garlic fractions stimulate B lymphocytes, the type of cells that produce antibodies.[6]

GARLIC AND MACROPHAGE FUNCTION

Phagocytes such as macrophages carry out their antimicrobial and antitumor activity by generating active oxygen intermediates during a process known as oxidative burst. We compared four garlic preparations and found that two of them enhance oxidative burst while the other two do not.[7] Product A in *Figure 15* is aged garlic extract which is same as Kyolic garlic extract.

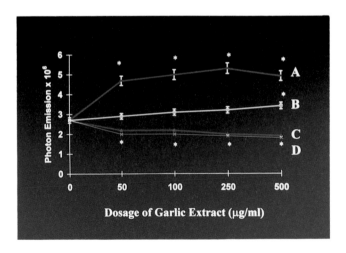

Figure 15. Comparison of the effects of four commercial garlic extracts on chemiluminescent oxidative burst in mouse peritoneal macrophages. Asterisks denote significant difference from the control without garlic treatment, $p < 0.05$.

GARLIC ENHANCES
T LYMPHOCYTE FUNCTION

Using hairless mice as a model, Dr. Vivienne Reeve and associates at the University of Sydney conducted an interesting study with this same aged garlic extract.[8] The hairless mice develop skin cancer when they are repeatedly exposed to ultra violet (UV) light radiation. UV light is known to be carcinogenic. Not only that. Previous study had shown UV light to cause accumulation of suppressor T lymphocytes to the site of irradiation. These suppressor cells suppress the immune response that normally will control the cancer growth.[9,10] The Australian investigators noted reddening and thickening of the skin when mice were exposed to the UV light. Animals fed 4% garlic in their diet had less skin thickening, showing that garlic extract protects animals from UV radiation damage. Mice exposed to UV light did not exhibit contact hypersensitivity due to immune suppression (UV light recruits suppressor T lymphocytes). Garlic feeding restored the contact hypersensitivity, showing that garlic augments T lymphocyte function in these animals.[8] Another study carried out by researchers at UCLA Medical School reports increase of interleukin-2, a cytokine made by helper T lymphocytes.[11] These studies substantiate our findings that garlic enhances cell mediated immunity.

HUMAN STUDIES

What about data on humans? Florida pathologist Dr. Tariq Abdullah and his associates tested the effect of garlic on natural killer cells of volunteer subjects.[12,13] Volunteers were divided randomly into three groups. The first took 0.5 gm/kg body weight of raw garlic every day for three weeks. The second group took 1800 mg of Kyolic (six capsules) every day for three weeks. The third group used no garlic and served as controls.

At the end of three weeks, researchers took blood samples from each volunteer and used the blood on tumor cells in a laboratory culture; they wanted to see how active each volunteer's natural killer cells worked against tumor cells. The natural killer cells of those who ate raw garlic killed 139 percent more tumor cells than the natural killer cells of those who did not eat garlic. The natural killer cells of those who took Kyolic capsules killed 159 percent more tumor cells than the natural killer cells of those who did not eat garlic. Incidentally, the Florida team believes that heat or cooking may destroy some of garlic's important constituents, so they chose Kyolic—the commercial garlic preparation that is not processed with heat.

Dr. Abdullah's group also carried out a pilot study involving ten AIDS patients who received garlic supplements for 12 weeks. With garlic supplementation there was an increase in natural killer cell activity and the helper-suppressor cell ratio, both signs of improved immune response. During the study period, the patients reported subjective improvement of their symptoms.[14]

CLINICAL OBSERVATION

In my medical practice, I see quite a number of patients with weakened immune function. Let me use the acronym **FAIL** to describe the signs and symptoms of a weakened immune system.

F for *frail and fragile*. These individuals are physically and emotionally weak. Any little disturbance can cause them to freak out.

A for *allergy of all kinds*. A person with a weakened immune function suffers from allergy which may be manifested in the form of skin rash and itching, gastrointestinal ailments such as indigestion, abdominal discomfort, gas, bloating, and respiratory symptoms such as scratchy throat and sinus problem.

I for *infections, particularly viral infections* manifested in the form of sore throat, muscle aches, low grade fever, and frequent colds.

L for *lethargy*. With low energy, these people feel tired all the time.

What causes weakened immune system? The answer is the **FAT CAT**. Of course I do not mean the real cat. I merely use these two words to depict the six most common factors that weaken the immune system.

F is food. High fat diet and refined sugars are known to lower the function of B lymphocytes, T lymphocytes, phagocytes, and natural killer cells.[15,16]

A for anxiety. A monograph titled *Psychoneuroimmunology*[17,18] documents that anxiety and stress depress all kinds of immune function.

T for toxicity. Toxic chemicals, heavy metals, and drugs (including both the prescription and many over-the-counter varieties) are known to impair the immune function.[19-21]

CAT refers to the three legalized drugs used by the general public, namely, **caffeine, alcohol,** and **tobacco**. Many scientific studies have documented the harmful effects of these legalized drugs on the immune system.[22-26]

In my clinical practice, I encourage my patients to avoid the **FAT CAT**. My wife is a dietitian who works closely with me in my office. She helps our patients to improve their overall nutrition. With a good nutritional program and stress management, many patients have been able to enjoy renewed immune function.

To conclude this chapter, I would say that all in all, accumulating scientific evidence suggests that components of garlic indeed modulate immunity. Our own clinical experience has further confirmed this to be true.

CHAPTER 9

FREE RADICAL PATHOLOGY

Today we hear and read a lot about antioxidants from the news media. Why antioxidants? We are told that antioxidants are used to combat the damaging effects of free radicals exerted on our bodies. Scientists believe that the antioxidant property is closely linked to the antiaging activity. Many think that for people who are young, antiaging may not be of an immediate concern. But I find even young people are interested in learning that antioxidants can keep them young, help them to look and feel good, and give them energy and endurance. Today, even exercise experts recommend that athletes keep up their stock of antioxidants to combat free radicals generated from athletic activities. For example, Dr. Kenneth Cooper, the physician who 30 years ago got Americans running recently wrote a book *Antioxidant Revolution*.[1] In his book, Dr. Cooper raises concern about the harm in vigorous exercise because of too much free radicals generated. He is now recommending moderate exercise with supplement of antioxidant nutrients for athletes.

FREE RADICALS AND MAJOR DISEASES

In this past decade we have come to recognize that many acute and chronic human sufferings are the results of excessive free radicals generated in our bodies. *Table 3* summarizes the major illnesses associated with free radicals.[2-7]

TABLE 3
Illnesses associated with free radicals

The Four Big 'A's:
Atherosclerosis,Aging,
Allergies,
AIDS

Blood Pressure

Cancer

Inflammatory Diseases (the '–itis'):
Arthritis, Bronchitis, Cystitis, Diverticulitis, etc.

Chronic Degenerative Diseases

First the four big 'A's: 1. Atherosclerosis or hardening of the artery, the underlying cause of heart attacks and strokes; 2. Aging—we are going to say more about that later on; 3. Allergies—I see more and more people suffering this problem; and 4. AIDS—the latest information indicates that free radicals render T lymphocytes susceptible to the damaging effects of human immunodeficiency virus (HIV). It has been suggested that if the antioxidant system in these cells is efficient, viruses cannot do much harm.[8-10]

Elevation of blood pressure is believed by some to be caused by too many free radicals that damage the blood vessels.[11,12]

More and more scientific data have pointed out that toxicity and reaction associated with free radicals are major causes of cancer, inflammatory and chronic degenerative diseases. Inflammatory diseases are those diseases which have "-itis" as part of their names, such as arthritis, bronchitis, cystitis, diverticulitis, esophagitis, etc. Some of these "itises" are due to infection, such as bronchitis caused by viruses, or cystitis (bladder infection) caused by bacteria. Other "itises" are associated with immune reactions, allergies, or lifestyle shortcomings. Many scientists now hold the position that the main cause of all these human sufferings listed in *Table 3* is from excess of free radicals.

WHAT ARE FREE RADICALS?

Free radicals, also called oxygen radicals, are highly reactive and unstable oxygen molecules. They have oxygen as a part of their structure with an extra unpaired electron. This electron causes them to eagerly bind with biological molecules such as lipid, protein, and nucleic acid in our body. Once they bind to the biological molecule, they will oxidize and damage these molecules. Examples of oxygen free radicals are superoxide with a structure formula O_2^-, hydrogen peroxide H_2O_2, hydroxyl $OH^\bullet$, and singlet oxygen $^1O_2$.

Under normal condition our body takes in oxygen and food to make energy in the form of adenosine triphosphate (ATP). During this process, normal amounts of free radicals are generated. Our body is endowed with an efficient antioxidant system that will either remove the excess free radicals or convert them into harmless substances such as water and oxygen to be recycled by the body. Vitamins such as ß-carotene, vitamin C and vitamin E are excellent free radical scavengers meaning they can remove or inactivate free radicals. Enzymes such as superoxide dismutase (SOD), catalase, and glutathione peroxidase, glutathione reductase, and methionine reductase can convert free radicals into harmless by-products.

Incidentally, small amounts of free radicals are actually beneficial to the body. To fight bacteria, viruses, and cancer cells, our immune cells (neutrophils and macrophages) use free radicals as ammunition. It is only when there are too many of them that we have trouble.

CAUSE OF EXCESS FREE RADICALS

What causes our bodies to have too many free radicals? The cause couldn't be stress, could it? It certainly could. Stress of our modern living is indeed the major cause of free radical pathology. What kind of stress are we talking about? There are four major types of stress: Physical, Chemical, Psychosocial, and Microbial (Infection).

Trauma or injury is an example of physical stress.

Chemical stress refers to the different kinds of chemicals we all are exposed to from time to time: heavy metals such as lead and mercury, pesticides, radioactive wastes, and various chemical drugs people take. Caffeine, alcohol, and tobacco (remember what we refer to as "CAT") are three legalized drugs many people indulge day to day and thus suffer this type of chemical stress as a result.

Psychosocial stress relates to interpersonal relationships with family members, coworkers, and others. Physical trauma and infection can bring about stress. As I mentioned before, free radicals are used by our body to fight infection. However, if there is an excessive amount, it may actually damage the surrounding tissue. In *Figure 16* it is shown that the normal balance between free radicals and antioxidant system is maintained. In *Figure 17* it is shown that the sum of stress-induced free radicals plus the normal amount of free

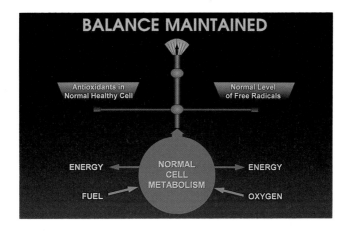

Figure 16. During the normal process of cellular metabolism, free radicals are generated. The antioxidant system in our body usually nullifies the harmful effects of free radicals and hence the balance is maintained.

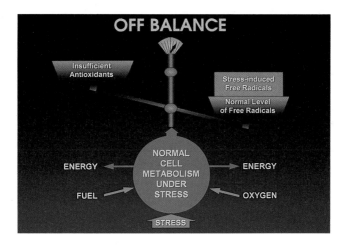

Figure 17. If our body is exposed to stress and the antioxidant system remains constant, the stress-induced free radicals will then cause the balance to be off.

radicals is too much for the normal amount of antioxidants to bear and hence the balance is OFF. What can we do to restore the balance?

We can do one of the two things. We can, first of all, reduce or eliminate the stress-induced free radicals. The second method is, of course, trying to replenish or supplement the supply of antioxidant store houses in our body. This is exactly why different companies try to convince us that we need to use their products.

ANTIOXIDANTS

Now, let us take a look at what antioxidants are. There are at least four main categories of antioxidants. 1. Antioxidant enzymes—superoxide dismutase (SOD), catalase, glutathione peroxidase and methionine reductase as mentioned before. These enzymes convert oxygen free radicals to harmless by-products. 2. Antioxidant vitamins (A, C, E)—serve as scavengers to remove free radicals. 3. Certain minerals such as selenium (Se) and zinc (Zn) are needed as coenzymes to enhance the activities of antioxidant enzymes. 4. The antioxidant phytochemicals (plant chemicals). Our laboratory has been studying these plant chemicals for the past 10 years[13]. We have learned that they work by enhancing and maximizing our body's antioxidant mechanisms. Speaking of selenium, garlic has a high concentration of this mineral in the organic form that our body can utilize.

We have studied a number of Chinese herbs and a hormone from the thymus gland,[14-21] more recently, we have studied garlic[22,23] using sophisticated in vitro (laboratory) models. In the next chapter, I am going to tell you what we and other researchers have discovered about garlic as an important antioxidant.

CHAPTER 10

ANTIOXIDANTS WHOSE TIME HAS COME

Lin Li, M.D., Ph.D., a postdoctoral fellow from the People's Republic of China, worked in my laboratory for three years. Her Ph.D. research focused on the role of the thymus gland in the aging process. She demonstrated that surgical removal of the thymus gland causes experimental animals to age very rapidly.[1-4] She was able to reverse the aging process by giving the animals thymic peptides (hormone from the thymus of young animal). She also found that phytochemicals from certain Chinese herbs were capable of doing the same, namely, retarding aging and/or restoring youthfulness.[5] The thymus gland has been known for years to regulate immune functions. Dr. Li's findings are significant in that she is one of the few who discovered the role of the thymus gland in the aging process. When she came to our laboratory, I encouraged her to continue her anti-aging study but suggested that she uses in vitro (laboratory) models instead of animals for her investigation.

Dr. Li succeeded in developing a model using tissue culture of artery endothelial cells (the type of cells that line the wall of blood vessels). With this model she utilized three assays to check the damage of blood vessel endothelial cells induced by the oxygen free radical. She chose to use hydrogen peroxide as the free radical.

The three assays are lactic dehydrogenase (LDH) release, which measures the integrity of cell membrane; MTT, a dye that measures the cell viability and the activity of mitochondria— organelles important for respiration of these cells. The purpose of the third assay is to measure lipid peroxidation resulting from free radical reaction. With this model Dr. Li demonstrated that the thymus hormone and several Chinese herbs can protect blood vessel endothelial cells from oxidation damage induced by a common free radical, hydrogen peroxide.[6-9] In addition to publishing these findings we decided to write a paper describing this model and published it in a journal specializing in In Vitro (in the test-tube) techniques.[10] We were gratified to see this paper generated so much interest. Researchers from all over the world wrote to us requesting reprints of this paper and many of them are now using this model for their antioxidant research. It is apparent that other researchers are also trying to get away from using whole animals for their studies.

Dr. Li's in vitro model intrigued one of our own research associates in the lab. Takeshi Yamasaki, D.V.M., M.S., the post-doctoral fellow from Japan, who was at this time working on the anticarcinogenic effect of garlic compounds, decided to test the antioxidant effect of garlic using this model. The results were gratifying in that we found aged garlic extract and one of its major constituents, S-allyl-cysteine, to also protect blood vessel endothelial cells from oxidation damage induced by hydrogen peroxide. This work was published in *Phytotherapy Research*.[11]

Figure 18 shows that when PAEC (pulmonary artery endothelial cells) were exposed to hydrogen peroxide, there was an increase of LDH release indicating the damage of cell membrane caused by hydrogen peroxide. If the cells were pretreated with aged garlic extract (AGE) and then exposed to hydrogen peroxide, there was very little release of LDH showing that AGE protected the cells from oxidative damage.

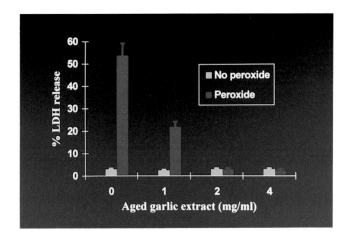

Figure 18. Effect of aged garlic extract (AGE) on hydrogen peroxide (H_2O_2)-induced release of LDH. Pulmonary artery endothelial cells were preincubated with AGE for 24 hours, washed, and exposed to H_2O_2 or buffer saline (as control) for 3 hours. Percent of LDH was then measured. Asterisk denotes significant difference ($p < 0.05$) from the control without AGE pretreatment.

Figure 19 shows that without hydrogen peroxide treatment, there was a high level of MTT indicating that cells were living. With hydrogen peroxide, there was a decrease of MTT indicating cells were damaged. Pretreating cells with AGE prevented the damage.

We mentioned that garlic can prevent oxidation of lipids. This is illustrated in *Table 4*. Hydrogen peroxide caused increase of lipid peroxide as indicated by thiobarbituric acid reactive substances (TBARS). Pretreating cells with aged garlic extract significantly inhibited the lipid peroxidation.

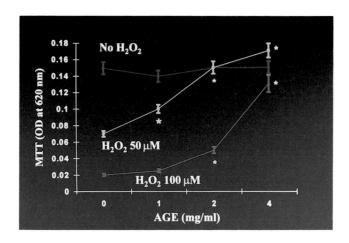

Figure 19. Effect of aged garlic extract (AGE) on hydrogen peroxide (H2O2)-induced cell damage. Pulmonary artery endothelial cells were preincubated with AGE for 24 hours, washed, and exposed to H2O2 or buffer saline (as control) for 3 hours. After washing, cell viability was measured by MTT assay. Asterisk denotes significant difference (p < 0.05) from the control without AGE pretreatment.

Before discussing our latest study with the aged garlic extract, let me first review for you the Glutathione Redox (Reduction-Oxidation) Cycle. Glutathione (GSH) is an important antioxidant chemical in our body. It helps enzyme GSH peroxidase to convert free radicals such as peroxides to harmless molecules such as water. In this process, GSH is oxidized to GSSG or the disulfide form. Our body has another enzyme called GSSG reductase. The name indicates that it is an enzyme that will reduce GSSG back to GSH *(see Figure 20)*.

TABLE 4
Effects of aged garlic extract (AGE) on hydrogen peroxide-
induced lipid peroxidation in pulmonary artery endothelial
cells (PAEC)

Pretreatment	H_2O_2 (µM)	TBARS (pmol)	% inhibition
None	0	1.97±0.90	—
None	50	30.23±1.74	0
AGE (1 mg)	50	20.83±1.11*	30.1
AGE (2 mg)	50	3.20±0.09*	89.4
AGE (4 mg)	50	4.49±1.34*	85.1

AGE was incubated with PAEC for 24 hours, removed by washing before exposing cells to hydrogen peroxide (H_2O_2) for 3 hours.

* *denotes significant difference from control exposed to H_2O_2 but without AGE pretreatment ($p < 0.05$).*

A study conducted by another Chinese postdoctoral fellow, Dr. Zhaohui Geng, shows that aged garlic extract can increase the level of GSH in the cells and at the same time it decreases the level of GSSG, the oxidized form of glutathione. It increases the activity of the enzyme GSSG reductase. We believe the reason that garlic increases GSH level is because of GSSG reductase. In addition, garlic also increases the activity of another antioxidant enzyme called superoxide dismutase (abbreviated as SOD) in the cells.[12] SOD is an important enzyme that neutralizes the effect of superoxide free radical.

Other researchers have also studied the antioxidant effects of

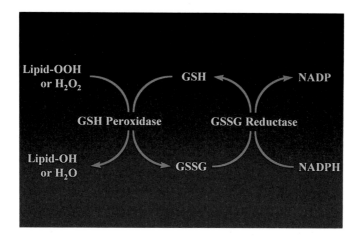

Figure 20. Glutathione (GSH) Redox (reduction-oxidation) cycle maintains the balance of intracellular oxidants and antioxidants.

garlic. Dr. Horie and associates in Japan have demonstrated that aged garlic extract protects liver cell membrane from lipid peroxidation.[13] They identified five sulfur-containing compounds in the garlic extract with potent antioxidant activity.[14] Further studies showed that garlic compounds act like scavengers capable of disposing free radicals.[15,16] Another garlic product, Kwai, has also been reported to have antioxidant activity.[17-19] Interestingly, studies have also revealed that raw garlic may increase the lipid oxidation indicating that some compounds in raw garlic may actually act like oxidants rather than antioxidants.[15,16]

Here is another interesting study showing the antioxidant effect of aged garlic extract using a unique experimental model. Doxorubicin or adriamycin is an anti-cancer drug. The main side effect is toxicity to the heart. The toxicity is due to oxidative stress—stress associated with free radicals. These researchers showed that aged garlic extract (AGE) can nullify the toxicity to the heart induced by doxorubicin.[20]

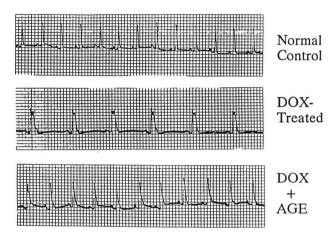

Normal Control

DOX-Treated

DOX + AGE

Figure 21. Electrocardiogram (EKG) tracing showing the effect of aged garlic extract on doxorubicin-induced cardiac damage. *From Kojima et al. with permission.*

Figure 21 is an electrocardiogram tracing. The upper tracing is normal. Note the short intervals between the peaks. The middle tracing represents animals treated with doxorubicin. We see the widening of the R-R intervals indicating that the heart muscle is injured. The bottom tracing represents animals treated with AGE and doxorubicin. The pattern here is the same as the normal animals indicating that garlic protects animals from doxorubicin toxicity.

We now know that the antioxidant activity is closely linked

with the immune function, and together, these mechanisms may account for the anti-aging property of garlic that I am eager to share with you in the next chapter.

CHAPTER 11

ANTI-AGING STUDIES

From the days of antiquity, men and women have been searching for the fountain of youth. Billions of dollars spent annually in this quest have resulted in a profitable market of foods, vitamins, potions, exercise paraphernalia, and anything else that promises escape from that enemy of all time—aging.

This preoccupation with anti-aging has invaded the research laboratory as well. Today scientists are attempting to discover ways in which to retard the aging process. Many believe that the antioxidant property, which was discussed in the previous chapter, is closely linked to anti-aging activity.[1,2]

The role of antioxidants in combating free radicals (elements in the body that damage the cells and thereby promote aging) is receiving widespread recognition. My own interest in antioxidants stems from extensive research with garlic. So I was particularly interested in knowing that people who enjoy longevity happen to be garlic lovers as well.

Here are some examples.

Dr. Bessie Delany, a 103-year-old retired dentist, lives with her 105-year-old sister Sarah Delany, a retired school teacher, in

Mount Vernon, New York.[3] The centenarian sisters are physically active. They cook their own meals, exercise daily, and take care of their home with the aid of an 80-year-old "youngster" who comes in once a week to help with the cleaning. Asked the secret of their longevity, the sisters answered: "Exercise is very important; we also watch our diet—staying away from fatty foods, eating as many as seven different vegetables a day, *and taking a clove of garlic every day.*"

Dr. Bernard Jensen in his new book *Garlic Healing Powers*[4] mentions two women he met while traveling in Armenia. The older woman was 128 years of age and was the mother of the young woman who was 85 years of age. These women credited their good health and longevity to eating garlic regularly. It appears that informed centenarians believe in the health benefit of garlic. Does garlic contribute to longevity?

In the previous chapter we mentioned that free radicals, especially oxygen radicals have been implicated in a variety of biological processes, not the least of which is aging.[5,6] While it has not yet been conclusively determined whether free radicals are a cause or an effect of aging, it is clear that characteristic types of free radical damage increase with age. According to the free radical theory of aging, the antioxidant defense system is weakened along with an increase in age, causing accumulation of free radicals in the body.[5]

The question to be asked is "will replenishing of antioxidants possibly restore youthfulness to an aged person?" Garlic has been shown to be an antioxidant,[7-10] and has various properties that protect against atherosclerosis[11,12] and enhance immune function.[13,14]Atherosclerosis and the decline of immune function are factors closely linked with the aging process. It is, therefore, only natural for researchers to look into the effect of garlic on aging parameters.[15]

A meeting of international garlic researchers was held in Washington, DC a year ago. Chinese and Japanese scientists presented some very exciting data in this meeting showing aged garlic extract extends lifespan and also restores memory loss in aged animals. Three studies have now been published.[16-18]

ANTI-AGING MODELS

For the past 25 years, Japanese investigators headed by Professor Toshio Takeda at the Kyoto University have developed special strains of mice for aging research. They call their animals "senescence accelerated mice" or SAM. One strain of mice age particularly quickly, and have a life span of nine to ten months; this strain is designated SAM-P for "senile prone." Another SAM strain lives for 16–18 months, twice as long as SAM-P, and is designated SAM-R for "senile resistant."

Incidentally, these mice were originally raised in the US and shipped to Japan some years ago. The main protein source for these mice is milk protein or casein as animals are fed in the US. One interesting and also significant incident was when the Japanese researchers put some of these mice on soy protein (the type of protein used predominantly in Asian countries) the animals actually lived 50% longer. The message here is, if one eats more soy beans instead of milk protein, one will live longer.

Feeding experiments were carried out with 2% aged garlic extract in the diet for a period of nine months.[16] The results show that garlic increased life span of senile prone rats (SAM-P) but had no significant effect on senile resistant rats (SAM-R).

Another study from the University of Tokyo deals with the effect of garlic on learning ability and memory retention.[17]

One of the several models used by the researchers to study the effects of garlic on learning and memory is an animal cage with an electric wire floor. A rubber pad is placed on top of the floor. As long as the animal stays on the rubber pad, the animal will not get shocked. But if the animal goes off the rubber pad, it will get an electric shock. Young animals tend to get off from the rubber pad. But they quickly learn not to do it again. Sometimes for curiosity reason, they may step onto the wire floor and get shocked more than one time. But usually they learn the lesson. Old senile mice, however, do not remember their mistakes, often stepping onto the wire floor several times within a short interval.

Ingestion of garlic extract did not affect normal young mice; they made an average of only two mistakes. Really, they should not have made two mistakes. One was probably enough. As I said before, young mice sometimes do that because of curiosity. With the SAM-P mice (the senile prone mice), they made an average of five mistakes of getting off the rubber pad and getting shocked. However, when these senile mice were given a garlic supplement in their diet, the error was reduced to a little over two times, almost like the young control mice. This experiment shows the efficacy of garlic in learning and memory retention in mice.

Figure 22 shows the effect of garlic supplement on memory. Again garlic did not affect the young mice but did affect the senile mice. Without garlic, the old mice just continued to get off the rubber pad and get shocked again and again. With garlic feeding, they now remembered to remain on the rubber pad just like the young mice. The third group of mice had their thymus removed. They aged very quickly (this was previously reported by Dr. Li before with her studies) so as to behave like old mice. It is interesting to note that feeding with garlic restored their memory as well.[18]

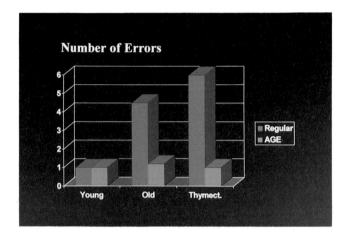

Figure 22. Effect of garlic on memory. Garlic feeding did not affect the memory of young mice but it did improve the memory of old and thymectomized mice after feeding these mice garlic for five months. *Adapted from Zhang et al. with permission.*

ALZHEIMER DISEASE

Some preliminary reports from China and Japan have suggested that some Alzheimer patients have been helped by garlic supplement.

I got acquainted with a retired dietitian several years ago. She lives in New York and visits retirement centers and nursing homes from time to time. One of her favorite gifts to her friends in these facilities for the elderly is garlic pills. For several years now, this dietitian vows to me that her friends in the nursing homes become more alert and active when taking garlic. Several nurses who work in the geriatric facilities have also reported to me that they have found that elderly persons benefit emotionally and intellectually from taking garlic. I have only limited clinical experience in this area. So far I have recommended garlic to a few Alzheimer patients. Although the results have been promising, the numbers of patients are too small to draw any scientific conclusion. I have talked to some of my former students who specialize in geriatrics about doing some controlled studies. So far none has been excited with my proposal. Maybe some day some one will be serious about this topic. Meanwhile, do you remember 103-year-old Dr. Bessie Delany and her 105-year-old sister Sarah I mentioned at the beginning of this chapter? If you don't remember, you know what to do. Take garlic and see if it will improve your memory.

CHAPTER 12

STRESS FIGHTER

We are living in a world full of stress. Nearly all the patients who consult my office will, sooner or later, confide to me that they are under a lot of stress. I learned early in my practice that my willingness to listen to their problems was vital for their recovery from illness, and that unless the stress level is reduced, it is futile to expect full restoration of physical health. In other words, as long as a patient is under stress, he is in distress. There are many papers now documenting that stress impairs our immune system, making it difficult for us to fight infection and even cancer.[1-4] Different people may be exposed to different kinds of stresses: environmental, physical, and psychosocial are some of the major ones. Environmental factors: noise, living condition, air, odor, extremes of temperature, can all bring stress to an individual. Other individuals may suffer stress because of certain physical discomforts or certain mechanical factors. Still others are victimized by psychosocial stress related to interpersonal relationships with family members, coworkers, and others. It is probably safe to say that every one of us, at one time or another, experiences stress at various degrees. Stress is not necessarily detrimental. A certain amount of stress is necessary to motivate us to do our very best. So stress can actually be very beneficial if managed effectively. Now what does garlic have to do with stress?

PHYSICAL STRESS

Several papers have been published by Dr. Tohru Fuwa and associates in Japan describing the effect of garlic on stress.[5-7] In one study the researchers randomly divided mice into three groups. The first group was subjected to cold temperatures (environmental stress); the second group was put in a box that was mounted on an oscillator that shook the box at 129 cycles per minute for four hours (physical stress). The third group was subjected to rope climbing (also a physical stress). Researchers noted that the stresses caused the mice to behave abnormally; all suffered loss of motor coordination, extreme fatigue, and loss of appetite.

Half of the mice were then given aged garlic extract, and the experiment was repeated. Those who ate the garlic were able to maintain motor coordination, recover more rapidly from fatigue, and function more efficiently than those who did not eat garlic.

PSYCHOSOCIAL STRESS

In another study, the researchers restrained a group of mice for twelve hours a day for four consecutive days—an experiment designed to mimic the effects of psychosocial stress. At the end of four days, the mice showed markedly reduced weight of the spleen and thymus and markedly fewer B lymphocytes with which to fight infection. In other words, researchers found that stress can impair the function of the immune system. When part of the mice were supplemented with garlic extract, no weight loss occurred and the optimum number of B lymphocytes was restored, boosting the immune system.

IMPROVED ENDURANCE

One of the main symptoms of stress, regardless of its source, is lack of energy; the victim of stress tires easily, becomes depressed, lacks motivation, and is filled with dread. In animal studies, stress causes a loss of strength and reduces endurance. A group of Indian investigators tested the effects of garlic on stress-crippled physical endurance to determine whether garlic could boost endurance.[8] Endurance for the study was measured by how long rats were able to keep swimming.

For the study, different groups of rats were given varying dosages of garlic juice or oil for a period of seven days; the control rats were given saline. Researchers then measured how long the rats could keep swimming before becoming too fatigued to continue. The rats were then injected with isoproterenol, a drug that damages the heart muscle, and swimming endurance was again measured.

The control rats—those who received only saline—swam for an average of 480 seconds before receiving the isoproterenol injection, and only 78 seconds after the injection. But the rats that had been fed garlic for seven days swam for an average of 840 seconds before and 560 seconds after the isoproterenol injection. This study demonstrated that 1) garlic boosts normal endurance (the rats fed garlic swam longer to begin with), and 2) garlic helps protect the rats even after their heart muscles had been damaged by isoproterenol.

Researchers at the Nihon University Medical School in Japan tested the effect of aged garlic extract in 20 college athletes undergoing one-month intense physical training.[9] Ten of these students took the aged garlic extract while the other ten took a placebo. Their results revealed that garlic supplement was clearly more effective than the placebo in preventing exhaustion and promoting recovery from the intense physical training. As I analyzed the findings of this study, I am reminded that Egyptian pharaohs prescribed extra rations of garlic to builders working on the massive pyramids to help enhance strength and endurance.

OUR OWN STUDY WITH STRESS

In an effort to measure garlic's effects on stress, my associates and I tested mice with Moloney sarcoma virus (MSV) induced tumors. Simply stated, we used a "stress machine" to test the mice that had MSV tumors. Our stress machine, developed by a Seattle-based microbiologist, was a modified phonograph that had the capacity to turn at various speeds. We placed the mice on top of the machine and rotated it at 45 rpms for ten minutes every hour. One group of mice was fed a regular laboratory diet. The second group was fed the same diet supplemented with 25 mg per day of garlic powder.

At the end of a week, we measured the levels of blood corticoid—the "stress hormone" that is secreted by the body when an animal or human is under stress. The mice on a regular diet had blood corticoid levels of 500 ng/ml, whereas those who took garlic supplements had dramatically lower levels of 100 ng/ml—only one-fifth the stress hormone *(see Figure 23)*. After the third week, we measured tumor volume in the two groups of mice. Those on a regular diet showed a progressive increase in the size of tumors; those who ate garlic had growth of tumors until the third week, after which there was a slow but steady reduction in the size of tumors *(see Figure 24)*.

CLINICAL STUDIES ON STRESS

I would now like to cite three clinical studies showing the impact of garlic on stress. In the first, more than a thousand patients in seven university-teaching hospitals including those at Hiroshima and Tokyo Universities were tested to determine whether garlic extract affected psychosomatic complaints. Each patient was given 2 ml of aged garlic extract every day for four weeks. At the end of the four-week test period, 50 to 80 percent of the patients who ate garlic experienced less fatigue, depression, and anxiety.[10]

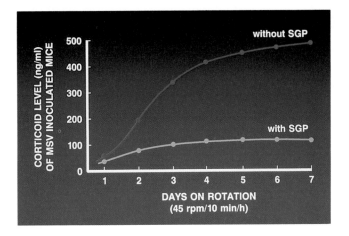

Figure 23. Effect of SGP (special garlic preparation) on "stress hormone". Animals subjected to hourly rotation as a form of physical stress (red circle) had steady increased levels of corticoid, whereas feeding with SGP significantly minimized this increase.

The second study involved patients with gynecological malignancies who underwent radiotherapy and/or chemotherapy.

Those patients who took two capsules of Kyolic a day for 30 to 270 days enjoyed significantly fewer side effects from the radiotherapy and chemotherapy. In fact, 67 percent of the women who took Kyolic reported having absolutely no side effects while they were taking their regular therapy.[11]

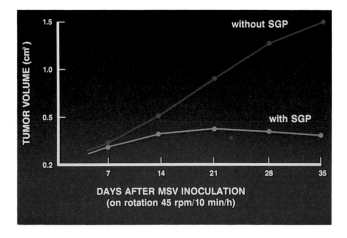

Figure 24. The increase in corticoid in Figure 23 is correlated with progressive increase in tumor volume. Animals supplemented with SGP had slow and minimal rise of tumor volume. Is it because they could cope better with stress?

The third study involved two groups of hospitalized patients. The first group of 20 patients took four capsules of garlic a day for 50 days; the control group took a placebo for the same period.[12] At the end of the test period, the garlic group showed more rapid recovery from exhaustion, had fewer complaints of fatigue after manual labor, and reported less feeling of cold in the extremities than did the placebo group. Interestingly, those over 50 years of age benefited more from the garlic in terms of endurance, possibly because younger patients had a higher reserve of energy.

GARLIC IMPROVES BLOOD CIRCULATION

An interesting study, carried out by physicians in the Second Hospital of Tokyo Women's Medical College, looked into the effect of the aged garlic extract on blood circulation.[13] Subjects were those with poor circulation and complaints of cold hands and feet. They also suffered pain and numbness of extremities and back. Subjects received two daily doses of one ml of garlic extract for one month. Using thermography to check the skin temperature as an objective measurement, the researchers found that the garlic supplement improved blood circulation, especially in the hands and feet. In this study, two-thirds of the elderly patients reported improvement of cold hands and feet, low back pain, and overall emotional outlook. Garlic supplement also reduced their levels of stress and fatigue.

Another recent study looking into the effect of garlic extract on peripheral circulation was carried out by Dr. Taneomi Okuhara of the Hiroshima City Hospital.[14] Subjects took a single dose of 1.6 ml of aged garlic extract. Thermographic measurement was made before, and at 30-minute intervals after garlic ingestion. Increased temperature in the hands was noted at 30 minutes which persisted for two hours. When subjects took garlic supplement every day for two weeks, there was a sustained improvement of blood circulation in both hands and feet (see Figure 25).

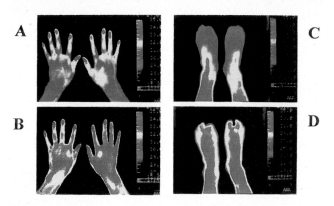

Figure 25. A and C are thermograms showing poor microcirculation of hands and feet, respectively, before the subject was given garlic supplement. B and D are thermograms of hands and feet showing improved microcirculation after the subject received two daily doses of 0.8 ml of garlic extract for 14 days. From Okuhara with permission.

CHAPTER 13

CANDIDA—
FRIEND OR FOE

In the past 10 years, several high school students have conducted experiments in my lab showing that fresh garlic inhibited bacteria, fungi, and viruses. These experiments are easy to perform and the youngsters were thrilled to see the results of their experiments. Several of them went on to win prizes in their science fairs.

Of the different fungi (molds and yeasts) the champion is *Candida albicans*, in terms of popularity. Several books have appeared describing the miserable conditions implicated with this yeast organism.[1-4] A number of individuals inflicted with the *Candida* problem have found relief from taking the aged garlic extract.

Some of these individuals have taken nystatin and raw garlic for controlling *Candida*. They did not like nystatin as they sometimes got quite sick with the medication. The same type of reaction also occurs with using raw garlic. Apparently, when nystatin or raw garlic kills the *Candida* organisms, there is a toxic reaction due to the release of toxic products from the dead yeast organisms. People refer to this as the "die off reaction," meaning dying of the yeast organisms with release of toxic chemicals to the body system.

Our research has largely dealt with the aged garlic extract called Kyolic. Earlier in our study, we discovered that Kyolic garlic extract does not kill *Candida* organisms directly. In a series of experiments, one of my graduate students found out that Kyolic garlic extract eliminated *Candida albicans* organisms from the blood and kidneys of animals not by directly killing these organisms. Rather, Kyolic extract enhanced the function of the animal's phagocytes. It is these phagocytes that actually eliminated the yeast organisms.[5]

THE TWO FACES OF CANDIDA

We have known for years, that *Candida* organisms are part of the normal flora that exist as an oval-shaped, budding yeast form in the human body. When *Candida* organisms take on an elongated shape, they then invade the host tissue to cause trouble *(see Figure 26)*. Unfortunately, some antibiotics and hormones cause this very thing to happen. This is why people occasionally develop *Candida* thrush (white cottage cheese like sores in the mouth) or vaginitis as side effects when taking certain antibiotics.

We are able to grow both the oval-shaped and elongated *Candida* yeasts in the laboratory. Using either human or rabbit serum, the oval yeast forms of *Candida* will start to convert to the elongated form in a couple hours if left alone. If we grow the yeast form of *Candida* in swine serum, the transformation from the oval shape to the elongated form will take place even faster and more complete. In a matter of 30 minutes nearly 100 percent of the yeast form will turn into the elongated form. In one of the experiments, I grew the yeast form of *Candida* organisms in swine serum. One sample was incubated with 2% Kyolic garlic, and another sample without Kyolic as the control. I was quite surprised to find an hour later, none of the budding yeast organisms had turned into elongated form in the presence of Kyolic garlic while all the *Candida* organisms in the control sample without Kyolic had all turned into elongated form. Now I understand Kyolic garlic does have an effect on *Candida* organisms. It does not kill the organisms, but it does prevent the organisms from transforming into the elongated invasive form. This may explain why people get the benefit of controlling the *Candida* problem without having to suffer the toxic symptoms associated with the "die off reaction."

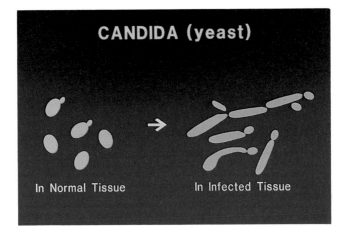

Figure 26. The two faces of *Candida albicans*. In the healthy tissue, the organisms appear as oval budding yeast cells as a part of the normal flora without causing trouble. Predisposing factors such as antibiotics, hormones, alcohol, and refined sugars can convert the oval form into the elongated form that is invasive.

A report regarding *Candida* organisms made by a professor of Kuwait University intrigued me. This study showed that in order for *Candida* yeasts to cause trouble in the mouth, they must first attach to the surface of the epithelial lining. The Kuwait professor demonstrated that garlic extract prevented yeasts from adhering to the buccal epithelial cells inside the mouth.[6]

In this past decade, I have seen a fairly large number of patients suffering so called "yeast syndrome." I do not use nystatin as some other physicians do. Instead, I use dietary changes, particularly, reducing the refined sugars. Use of garlic supplement often ties them over the difficult time. I also help them with stress management. Many of these patients are now symptom free and have been able to enjoy their renewed health.

CHAPTER 14

CONCLUSION— THE TRIANGLE OF DISEASE

Dear Reader, I have enjoyed communicating with you through these pages, and I hope you have enjoyed reading them. In concluding this book, I would like to share with you a concept that I have used in my teaching for a number of years. So please sit back, relax, and pretend you are in an auditorium with 150 or more of my students. The class has just begun. My energetic students have their eyes wide open wondering what knowledge their teacher has to convey to them today. The concept is called "The Triangle of Disease." I usually will flash on the screen a slide showing the triangle which you can now see on *Figure 27.*

The disease process can be illustrated using this triangle. The three angles are: the etiology (Webster defines it as "the assignment of a cause or reason"), the susceptible host, and predisposing factors. If we use infection as an example, the three angles are: 1) microbes as the etiologic agent, 2) a susceptible host or a person who is susceptible because of impaired immunity, impaired phagocytic function, poor nutrition and/or a risky lifestyle determining the susceptibility, and 3) certain factors such as trauma, toxic exposure, stress and underlying disease which predispose a person to infection.

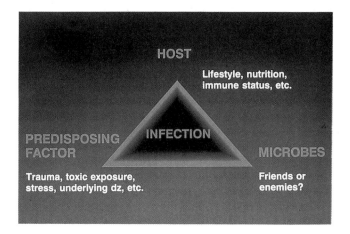

Figure 27. The triangle of infection is used to illustrate the three aspects of a disease process.

Looking at the triangle, one needs to recognize that microorganisms alone do not usually cause infection unless there is a susceptible host, even though we give the textbook definition of infection as an invasion of the body by microorganisms. The concept that I want to emphasize is that microorganisms alone do not usually cause infection unless there is a susceptible human being or animal. Having said that, let me hasten to add that even with a susceptible host and the presence of microbes, there still may not be an infection unless the process is triggered by certain predisposing factors. For this reason, in the prevention or treatment of an infectious disease, we need to look at all three angles rather than just one of these angles. Merely killing the microbes may not be the best solution. Indeed often carried with it is the price of unwanted side effects. Typical examples are yeast infections such as *Candida* oral thrush and *Candida* vaginitis following the use of a broad spectrum antibiotic.

In the case of infection we obviously need to consider the microbes as the primary factor, and the host and predisposing factors as secondary factors. However, it is equally important to bear in mind when considering a disease that all three angles have equal weight or significance. An example of a clinical entity I often use with my medical students is diarrhea. It has been estimated that in the world each day there are 20 million people suffering from diarrhea. We all know that often our diarrhea is simply due to eating the wrong kind of food. In other words, it may not have anything to do with the microbes. In the figure under microbes, I have "friends or enemies." The point is that it may not be easy to know which microbe is the enemy and which is the friend. For example, a person eats the wrong kind of food and has diarrhea. If he consults a physician and gets a course of antibiotic, he will then be killing friendly bacteria without touching the enemy at all, since there may not be any enemy to begin with.

Looking at the third angle, the predisposing factors, it is my practice to constantly remind my students that this angle is a very important one. It too may be the primary cause of a complaint, rather than secondary. Again, take the complaint of diarrhea. It is true that we do not want to miss those germs like *Salmonella, Shigella, Campylobacter,* and *Vibrio* that are famous intestinal pathogens. What I want to remind my students is that before they write a prescription for a potent drug, find out and *study* what drugs the patient has been taking. In my own experience, I have seen case after case of patients complaining of diarrhea or other gastrointestinal discomfort due to one or more drugs received from a doctor. An assignment I have given my students is to check the *Physicians' Desk Reference* (PDR) to make a list of drugs without gastrointestinal side effects. The current PDR has more than 2000 pages. The lesson to be learned from this exercise is that there are very few drugs in the big book without gastrointestinal side effects! So let me make a short conclusive remark regarding the triangle: each of the three angles can have equal importance.

It is important to point out that this triangle and its basic principle applies not only to infection but also to most, if not all, major diseases inflicting the human race. For example, we can change the entity from infection to cancer and all we need to modify is just one of the triangles—adding chemical carcinogens and radiation to the microbes. We mentioned previously that the three best-known causes of cancer are carcinogens, radiation, and viruses. With that in mind, the prevention and treatment of cancer should thus encompass all three angles. Merely killing the viruses is not the solution. For that matter, current methods of focusing only at killing cancer cells is not adequate. One needs to strengthen the host and to remove the predisposing factor in order to obtain a satisfactory and lasting result.

What about AIDS? The same principle applies here. Every one has heard of the viral culprit—HIV or Human Immunodeficiency Virus blamed for AIDS. People are afraid of HIV, and justifiably so. But I need to remind all of us that there is the HOST— lifestyle, nutrition, and the immune status; and there are predisposing factors—toxic exposure such as recreational drugs, trauma, and stress. To prevent AIDS and to help individuals with HIV infection, we need to consider all the three angles.

Methods aimed at merely killing viruses are not useful. Whatever kills viruses most likely will also harm the cells which support the growth of the viruses. Billions of dollars have been spent to find a magic bullet to cure AIDS, but to no avail. We need to readjust our thinking and pay attention to this triangle of the disease. One needs to strengthen the host through lifestyle modification and proper nutrition. Oh, yes, predisposing factors, which are the most important, need to be removed. Drugs (recreational, "over the counter," prescription, legal, or illegal) and toxic materials that suppress the immune system can no longer be tolerated.

Can garlic be used to treat AIDS? That's a very difficult question; once the disease is fully developed, it is not likely that any single agent or approach will be effective in its treatment. That brings us to a second critical question: Can garlic possibly help prevent AIDS?

I think it can.

Why? Because, as I look at the triangle of disease, I recall all I have learned about garlic: Garlic can inhibit the growth of viruses,[1-4] garlic enhances the function of phagocytes, T lymphocytes, and natural killer cells,[5-7] and garlic nullifies some of the toxins that impair the immune system.[8] Viruses are parasites in the true sense as they are incapable of reproducing themselves. When a virus enters a cell, it uses its genes to direct the cell to make more viruses. To do so, viral genes must first be expressed. Our latest studies have revealed that garlic compounds can suppress the process of gene expression in the test tube,[9] most likely through its antioxidant mode of action. If this suppression can happen in the body, there will be no viral growth!

It thus appears that this natural product has all the good qualities to ensure a healthy host. For this reason, I believe it can be used to advantage together with a sound, healthful lifestyle to prevent a disease even as dreadful as AIDS.

Quite a few years ago, I came across a book entitled *The Ministry of Healing* written by Ellen G. White almost a century ago.[10]

I was impressed with a statement on page 127 of this book where she says, "In case of sickness, the cause should be ascertained. Unhealthful conditions should be changed, wrong habits corrected. Then nature is to be assisted in her effort to expel impurities and to re-establish right conditions in the system." Let's apply this statement to our triangle: In case of sickness (again, let's say in this case we are dealing with infection), we are to do five things:

1. Cause should be ascertained (not just the microbes but the whole triangle).

2. Unhealthful conditions should be changed (this means maybe we need to change our lifestyle).

3. Wrong habits should be corrected (including dietary habits).

4. Assist nature to expel impurities (such as toxic exposure).

5. Re-establish right conditions in the system (we need to cooperate with nature and allow our body to heal itself).

Maybe at this moment the question you have in your mind is "What does garlic have to do with this?" Please read point number four again. Garlic can help our bodies expel impurities. We have discussed in previous chapters that garlic detoxifies the system of heavy metal poisoning, protects against irradiation, and even kills microbes.

Looking at the triangle again, we see that components of garlic actually encompass all three angles. It is amazing that nature has provided us with such an "all around" product that is useful for one's health.

What about you? Have you done something today to keep the triangle balanced? If your answer is "not yet" or "not quite," it is time then to adjust your thinking and to begin a regular program that will enhance your health and well being. If your answer is "yes," then you are on your way to enjoying life's fullness! As you proceed on that wonderful journey, make sure you share these principles of healthful living with friends and loved ones—and together you'll discover nature's key to good health!

Recently, I made a presentation of our garlic research to 120 young pharmacists visiting California. At the end of my presentation, I used the word "GARLIC" as an acronym to summarize its major health benefits. Please allow me to use this acronym to conclude this book:

G - good for many things.

A - antioxidant effects.

R - restoration of memory.

L - life extension.

I - immune modulation.

C - cancer prevention.

Do not underestimate the value of this lowly bulb, especially when used in conjunction with a healthful lifestyle.

APPENDIX

ANSWERS TO MOST
FREQUENTLY ASKED QUESTIONS

Q. How much raw garlic can a person take, and how much will be considered adequate for health benefit?

A. Most people can take one or two cloves of raw garlic a day without problem. It has been estimated that one clove a day will provide sufficient amount of active ingredients for health benefits.

Q. When garlic is cooked, the pungent odor is less, but do I still get its benefit?

A. Yes, you would still get its benefits. Garlic contains many chemicals, some of them are heat labile while others are heat stable. Light cooking retains most of the active beneficial ingredients.

Q. Where can I buy odorless garlic products?

A. Odorless garlic products are sold in most health food stores, nutrition centers, and large supermarkets. Check the Yellow Page section of the telephone directory and call the stores before you go. Health food store personnel are usually very helpful and willing to give you specific information.

Q. How did you treat bladder cancer? Was garlic given by mouth or by bladder irrigation?

A To begin with, I want to mention that our work with bladder cancer was carried out in animals (mice). The garlic extract was given directly into the bladder and also injected systemically. Direct irrigation into the bladder gave much better results.

Q. Has garlic been used in treating human bladder cancer? Can you tell us which doctors are doing this kind of treatment?

A. I am not aware of any doctor who is treating human bladder cancer patients with garlic. To do so, the doctor needs to get FDA approval to conduct so-called "Phase One Study" first. I am not aware of any doctor or researcher has attempted to conduct such a study.

Q. How much garlic should one take?

A. An adult person can usually take one to two cloves of raw garlic a day without trouble. If you experience abdominal discomfort, that probably means you already have too much. Generally speaking, more can be taken if garlic is cooked. When I was in Europe, I enjoyed baked garlic served in some restaurants. The whole garlic bulb was baked in oven until it was browned. Just peel off the cloves and eat them that way. People eat two to three bulbs with no problems. In terms of commercial garlic products (capsules, pills, or tablets), it is best to follow the dosages recommended by the manufacturers. This is particularly true if the product is made of raw garlic as too much over the recommended dosage may cause discomfort. With Kyolic aged garlic, there has not been a problem with toxicity. People have taken four or five teaspoons of liquid garlic extract a day (equivalent to 20 to 25 capsules of powder) with no problem. However, more is not necessarily better. So do not over do it.

Q. Can garlic be taken together with other regular medications?

A. Garlic is a nutritional supplement. Generally speaking, moderate amount will not interfere with regular medications. However, since garlic does have pharmacological activity, for example, garlic has anticoagulant activity, it is wise for those who are on regular medications to consult their doctors before adding garlic supplement to the nutritional program.

Q. Some people get nauseated and have loose bowel when taking garlic. Do you have any advice as what they should do?

A. I believe that this usually happens when raw (fresh) garlic or a product containing raw garlic is taken. Raw garlic may kill some good intestinal bacteria and cause such complaints in individuals who are particularly sensitive. To avoid such discomfort, one can either reduce the dosage or choose a brand such as Kyolic. If one likes fresh garlic, slight cooking often will eliminate the irritating chemicals that cause nausea and loose bowel.

Q. Can children take garlic pills? How much should they take?

A. Garlic can be taken by people of all ages. Generally speaking, child's dosage is half of the adult's. For younger children, liquid form of garlic extract is more convenient.

Q. How many kinds of garlic products have you studied?

A. The first garlic product we studied is the Schilling Instant Garlic Powder, the kind you can get in any supermarket. We have also studied various brands which are available from the grocery stores and health food stores in addition to the fresh garlic. The major portions of our studies were carried out with the aged garlic extract from Japan.

Q. Do companies selling garlic products conduct research?

A. Yes, some of them do. The two companies that conduct extensive garlic research are Lichtwer Pharma GmbH, Berlin, Federal Republic of Germany (its products go by the name of Kwai) and Wakunaga Pharmaceutical Co. Ltd., Hiroshima, Japan (with trade name of Kyolic or Aged Garlic Extract).

Q. What is the difference between Kwai and Kyolic products?

A. Kwai is made of fresh garlic enclosed in a cellulose coating. Most people do not detect the odor of garlic although a few individuals report "garlic breath" shortly after taking it. Kyolic product is prepared by processing garlic in diluted alcohol solution for a period of several months. During this time, the irritating chemicals are converted to more bioavailable harmless compounds. This is essentially an "aging" process used by the Chinese for thousands of years to render garlic odorless.

Q. Are there differences between liquid and powdered forms of aged garlic extract? Have tests been performed to compare the effects of these two forms?

A. In general, there is not that much difference. For individuals with absorption problems, the liquid form is more readily absorbed and assimilated. Our initial studies were carried out with the liquid form. We have since used the powder form with very similar results.

Q. I am an athlete and have taken Kyolic garlic for many years. Recently, Dr. Kenneth Cooper feels that it is extremely important for athletes to protect themselves against free radical production. Will the garlic I take be adequate for this purpose?

A. I am fully in agreement with Dr. Cooper in recommending antioxidant supplement for athletes in addition to advising them to take plenty of fresh fruits and vegetables. Athletic activity requires a lot of energy expenditure and as a result there is generation of excess of free radicals. If you are an active athlete, garlic alone may not be adequate source of antioxidants. Since you already take Kyolic, I would like to recommend Kyolic formula 105 which contains ß-carotene, vitamins C and E, and selenium in addition to garlic extract. The vitamin E in this formula is alpha tocopherol succinate. In our experience, succinate is more bioavailable than acetate or citrate. Another good formula is GINKGO BILOBA PLUS which contains *Ginkgo biloba*, a potent antioxidant phytochemical, and Siberian ginseng which improves endurance, in addition to garlic extract. There appears to be synergistic effects of these ingredients.

Q. My nutritionist has recommended me to use Kyolic Formula 103. What is your opinion of this product?

A. It so happens that Formula 103 is also the product I often recommend to my patients as a general purpose supplement. This formula has vitamin C and a Chinese herb called

Astragalus membranaceus in addition to garlic extract. Vitamin C is a potent antioxidant, among other things. *Astragalus membranaceus* has been extensively studied by various investigators including our group. It is a strong immune modulator and is considered an important tonic in China.

REFERENCES

CHAPTER 1: Introduction

1. The American Collectors Association: Magnitude of healthcare collections. In *Surprising Facts about Healthcare Collection*, Spring issue, ACA, Minneapolis, MN, 1996.

2. Dentzer S: America's scandalous health care. US News and World Report 108:24, 1990.

3. Kinsella, KG: Changes in life expectancy 1900-1990. Am J Clin Nutr 55:1196S, 1992.

4. Lau BHS, Tadi PP, Tosk JM: *Allium sativum* (garlic) and cancer prevention. Nutr Res 10:937, 1990.

5. Lau BHS: Garlic for disease prevention. J Health Healing 13:3, 1990.

6. Lau BHS, Adetumbi MA, Sanchez A: *Allium sativum* (garlic) and atherosclerosis: a review. Nutr Res 3:119, 1983.

7. Lau BHS: Garlic For Health. Lotus Light Publications, Wilmot, WI, 1988.

8. Lau BHS: Garlic Research Update. Odyssey Publishing Inc. Vancouver, B.C., Canada, 1991.

CHAPTER 2: The Beginnings of Our Garlic Research

1. Fliermans CB: Inhibition of *Histoplasma capsulatum* by garlic. Mycopathol Mycol Appl 50:227, 1973.

2. Tansey MR, Appleton JA: Inhibition of fungal growth by garlic extract. Mycologia 67:409, 1975.

3. Appleton JA, Tansey MR: Inhibition of growth of zoopathogenic fungi by garlic extract. Mycologia 67:882, 1975.

4. Barone FE, Tansey MR: Isolation, purification, identification, synthesis, and kinetics of activity of the anticandidal components of *Allium sativum* and a hypothesis for its mode of action. Mycologia 69:793, 1977.

5. Fromtling R, Bulmer GS: In vitro effect of aqueous extract of garlic (*Allium sativum*) on the growth and viability of *Cryptococcus neoformans*. Mycologia 70:397, 1978.

6. Delaha EC, Garagusi VF: Inhibition of mycobacteria by garlic extract (*Allium sativum*). Antimicrob Agents Chemother 27:485, 1985.

7. Adetumbi MA, Lau BHS: Inhibition of in vitro germination and spherulation of *Coccidioides immitis* by *Allium sativum*. Current Microbiol 13:73, 1986.

8. Adetumbi MA, Javor GT, Lau BHS: *Allium sativum* (garlic) inhibits lipid synthesis by *Candida albicans*. Antimicrob Agents Chemother 30:499, 1986.

9. Ghannoum MA: Studies on the anticandidal mode of action of *Allium sativum* (garlic). J General Microbiol 134:2917, 1988.

10. Ghannoum MA: Inhibition of Candida adhesion to buccal epithelial cells by an aqueous extract of *Allium sativum* (garlic). J Appl Bacteriol 68:163, 1990.

11. Prasad G, Sharma VD: Efficacy of garlic (*Allium sativum*) treatment against experimental candidiasis in chicks. Brit Vet J 136:448, 1980.

12. Amer M, Taha M, Tosson Z: The effect of aqueous garlic extract on the growth of dermatophytes. Int J Dermatol 19:285, 1980.

13. Hunan Medical College, China. Garlic in cryptococcal meningitis. A preliminary report of 21 cases. Chinese Med J 93:123, 1980.

14. Tjia TL, Yeow YK, Tan CB: Cryptococcal meningitis. J Neurol Neurosurg Psych 48:853, 1985.

15. Tutakne MA, Bhardwaj JR, Satyanarayanan G, Sethi IC: Sporotrichosis treated with garlic juice. Indian J Dermatol 28:40, 1983.

16. Lu DP, Guo NL, Jin NR, Zheng H, Lu XJ, Shi Q: Allogeneic bone marrow transplantation for the treatment of leukemia. Chinese Med J 103:125, 1990.

17. Tsai Y, Cole LL, Davis LE, Lockwood SJ, Simmons V, Wild GC: Antiviral properties of garlic: In vitro effects on influenza B, herpes simplex and coxsackie viruses. Planta Medica 5:460, 1985.

18. Nagai K: Experimental studies on the preventive effect of garlic extract against infection with influenza virus. Japanese J Inf Dis 47:321, 1973.

19. Guo NL, Lu DP, Woods, GL, Reed E, Zhou GZ, Zhang LB, Waldman RH: Demonstration of the anti-viral activity of garlic extract against human cytomegalovirus in vitro. Chinese Med J 106:93, 1993.

20. Esanu V, Prahoveanu E: The effect of garlic extract, applied as such or in association with NaF, on experimental influenza in mice. Rev Roum Med Virol 34:11, 1983.

21. Chaudhury DS, Sreenivasamurthy V, Jayaraj P, Sreekantiah KR, Johar DS: Therapeutic usefulness of garlic in leprosy. J Indian Med Assoc 39:517, 1962.

22. Varon S: Medical student discovers curative powers of garlic. Heritage p. 28, April 10, 1987.

23. Mirelman D, Monheit D, Varon S: Inhibition of growth of *Entamoeba histolytica* by allicin, the active principle of garlic extract (*Allium sativum*). J Infect Dis 156:243, 1987.

24. Yoshida S, Kasuga S, Hayashi N, Ushiroguchi T, Matsuura H, Nakagawa S: Antifungal activity of ajoene derived from garlic. Appl Environ Microbiol 53:615, 1987.

25. Adetumbi MA, Lau BHS: *Allium sativum* (garlic) - a natural antibiotic. Med Hypotheses 12:227, 1983.

CHAPTER 3: Garlic and Blood Lipids

1. Lau BHS, Adetumbi MA, Sanchez A: *Allium sativum* (garlic) and atherosclerosis: a review. Nutr Res 3:119, 1983.

2. Qureshi AA, Din ZZ, Abuirmeileh N, Burger WC, Ahmad Y, Elson CE: Suppression of avian hepatic lipid metabolism by solvent extracts of garlic: impact on serum lipids. J Nutr 113:1746, 1983.

3. Qureshi AA, Abuirmeileh N, Din ZZ, Elson CE, Burger WC: Inhibition of cholesterol and fatty acid biosynthesis in liver enzymes and chicken hepatocytes by polar fractions of garlic. Lipids 18:343, 1983.

4. Lau BHS, Lam F, Wang-Cheng R: Effect of an odor-modified garlic preparation on blood lipids. Nutr Res 7:139, 1987.

5. Bordia A: Effect of garlic on blood lipids in patients with coronary heart disease. Am J Clin Nutr 34:2100, 1981.

6. Chang ML, Johnson MA: Effect of garlic on carbohydrate metabolism and lipid synthesis in rats. J Nutr 110:931, 1980.

7. Chi MS, Koh ET, Stewart TJ: Effects of garlic on lipid metabolism in rats fed cholesterol or lard. J Nutr 112:241, 1982.

8. Jain RC: Onion and garlic in experimental cholesterol atherosclerosis in rabbits. I. Effect of serum lipids and development of atherosclerosis. Artery 1:115, 1975.

9. Nakamura H, Ishikawa M: Effect of S-methyl-1-cysteine sulfoxide on cholesterol metabolism. Kanzo 12:673, 1971.

10. Kritchevsky D, Tepper SA, Morrisey R, Klurfeld D: Influence of garlic oil on cholesterol metabolism in rats. Nutr Reports Int 22:641, 1980.

11. Mader FH: Treatment of hyperlipidemia with coated garlic tablets. Double-blind study with 261 patients in 30 general practices. Deer Allgemeinarzt 8:435, 1990.

12. Vorberg G, Schneider B: Therapy with garlic: results of a placebo-controlled double-blind study. Br J Clin Pract Sym Suppl 69:7, 1990.

13. Warshafsky S, Kamer RS, Sivak SL: Effect of garlic on total serum cholesterol - a meta-analysis. Ann Intern Med 119:599, 1993.

14. Silagy C, Neil A: Garlic as a lipid lowering agent - a meta-analysis. J Royal College Physicians London 28:39, 1994.

CHAPTER 4: How Garlic Affects Lipid Metabolism

1. Castelli WP: Epidemiology of coronary heart disease. Am J Med 76: 4, 1984.

2. Stamler J, Wentworth D, Neaton JD: Is relationship between serum cholesterol and risk of premature death from coronary heart disease continuous or graded? Findings in 356,222 primary screenees of the multiple risk factor intervention trial (MRFIT). J Am Med Assoc 256:2823, 1986.

3. Shoetan A, Augusti KT, Joseph PK: Hypolipidemic effects of garlic oil in rats fed ethanol and a high lipid diet. Experientia 40:261, 1984.

4. Qureshi AA, Din ZZ, Abuirmeileh N, Burger WC, Ahmad Y, Elson CE: Suppression of avian hepatic lipid metabolism by solvent extracts of garlic: impact on serum lipids. J Nutr 113:1746, 1983.

5. Qureshi AA, Abuirmeileh N, Din ZZ, Elson CE, Burger WC: Inhibition of cholesterol and fatty acid biosynthesis in liver enzymes and chicken hepatocytes by polar fractions of garlic. Lipids 18:343, 1983.

6. Chang ML, Johnson MA: Effect of garlic on carbohydrate metabolism and lipid synthesis in rats. J Nutr 110:931, 1980.

7. Yeh YY, Yeh SM: Garlic reduces plasma lipids by inhibiting hepatic cholesterol and triacylglycerol synthesis. Lipids 29:189, 1994.

8. Itokawa Y, Inoue K, Sasagawa S, Fujiwara M: Effect of S-methylcysteine and related sulfur-containing amino acids on lipid metabolism of experimental hypercholesterolemic rats. J Nutr 103:88, 1973.

9. Chi MS: Effects of garlic products on lipid metabolism in cholesterol-fed rats. Proc Soc Exp Bio Med 171:174, 1982.

10. Adoga GI, Osuoi J: Effect of garlic oil extract on serum, liver and kidney enzymes of rats fed on high sucrose and alcohol diets. Biochem Int 13:615, 1986.

11. Lau BHS, Lam F, Wang-Cheng R: Effect of an odor-modified garlic preparation on blood lipids. Nutr Res 7:139, 1987.

12. Miller GJ, Miller NE: Plasma-high-density-lipoprotein concentration and development of ischaemic heart-disease. Lancet 1:16, 1975.

13. Carew TE, Hayes SB, Koschinsky T, Steinberg D: A mechanism by which high-density lipoproteins may slow the atherogenic process. Lancet 1:1315, 1976.

14. Steinberg D, Parthasarathy S, Carew TE, Khoo JC, Witztum JL: Beyond cholesterol. Modifications of low-density lipoprotein that increase its atherogenicity. New Eng J Med 320:915, 1989.

15. Steinberg D: Role of oxidized LDL and antioxidants in atherosclerosis. Adv Exp Med Biol 369:39, 1995.

16. Ide N, Nelson AB, Lau, BHS: Garlic compounds inhibit oxidation of LDL. Planta Medica 1996.

17. Phelps S, Harris WS: Garlic supplementation and lipoprotein oxidation susceptibility. Lipids 28:475, 1993.

18. Lewin G, Popov I: Antioxidant effects of aqueous garlic extract. 2nd communication: inhibition of the Cu^{2+}-initiated oxidation of low density lipoproteins. Arzneim Forsch 44:604, 1994.

CHAPTER 5: Other Risk Factors for Cardiovascular Diseases

1. Sassa H, Ito JT, Niwa T, Matsui E: Fibrinolysis in patients with ischemic heart disease. Japanese Circulat J 39:525, 1975.

2. Chakrabarti R, Hocking ED, Fearnley GR: Fibrinolytic activity and CAD. Lancet 1:987, 1968.

3. Lau BHS: Anticoagulant and lipid regulating effects of garlic (*Allium sativum*). In *New Protective Roles of Selected Nutrients in Human Nutrition*, Gene A. Spiller and James Scala, editors, Alan R. Liss, publisher, p. 295, 1989.

4. Sainani GS, Desai DB, Gorhe NH, Natu SM, Pise DV, Sainani PG: Dietary garlic, onion and some coagulation parameters in Jain community. J Asso Phys India 27:707, 1979.

5. Sainani GS, Desai DB, Gorhe NH, Natu SM, Pise DV, Sainani PG: Effect of dietary garlic and onion on serum lipid profile in Jain community. Indian J Med Res 69:776, 1979.

6. Sainani GS, Desai DB, More KN: Onion, garlic and atherosclerosis. Lancet 1:575, 1976.

7. Bolton S, Null G, Troetel WM: The medical uses of garlic - fact and fiction. Am Pharm 22:448, 1985.

8. Loeper M, Debray M: Antihypertensive action of garlic extract. Bull Soc Med 37:1032, 1921.

9. Piotrowski G: L'ail en therapeutique. Praxis 488, 1948.

10. Srinivasan V: A new antihypertensive agent. Lancet 2:800, 1969.

11. Barrie SA, Wright JV, Pizzorno JE: Effects of garlic oil on platelet aggregation, serum lipids and blood pressure in humans. J Orthomolecular Med 2:15, 1987.

12. McMahon FG, Vargas R: Can garlic lower blood pressure? A pilot study. Pharmacotherapy 13:406, 1993.

13. Zheziang Institute of Traditional Chinese Medicine: The effect of essential oil of garlic on hyperlipidemia and platelet aggregation. J Trad Chinese Med 6:117, 1986.

14. Petkov V: A pharmacological study of garlic (*Allium sativum* L.). Annuaire de l'Universite de Sofia, Faculte de Medecine, t. XXVIII 885, 1949.

15. Petkov V: On the action of garlic (*Allium sativum* L.) on the blood pressure. Sovremenna Medizina 1:5, 1950.

16. Petkov V: New experimental data about the pharmacodynamics of some plant species. Sofia: Nauka i Iskustve 227, 1953.

17. Petkov V: Uber die Pharmakodynamik einiger in Bulgarien wildwashsender bzw angebauter Arzneipflanzen. Zeitschreift fur arztliche Fortbildung 56:430, 1962.

18. Petkov V, Stoev V, Bakalov D, Petev L: The Bulgarian drug Satal as a remedy for lead intoxication in industrial conditions. Higiena Truda i Profesionalnie Zabolevania 4:42, 1965.

19. Petkov V: Plants with hypotensive, antiatheromatous and coronarodilatating action. Am J Chinese Med 3:197, 1979.

20. Siegel G, Walter A, Schnalke F, Schmidt A, Buddecke E, Loirand G, Stock G: Potassium channel activation, hyperpolarization, and vascular relaxation. Z Kardiol 80 Suppl 7:9, 1991.

21. Agel MB, Gharaibah MN, Salhab AS: Direct relaxant effects of garlic juice on smooth and cardiac muscles. J Ethnopharmacol 33:13, 1991.

22. Das I, Khan NS, Sooranna SR: Potent activation of nitric oxide synthase by garlic: a basis for its therapeutic applications. Curr Med Res Opin 13:257, 1995.

23. Das I, Khan NS, Sooranna SR: Nitric oxide synthase activation is a unique mechanism of garlic action. Biochem Soc Trans 23:136S, 1995.

24. Koshland Jr DE: The molecule of the year [editorial]. Science 258:1861, 1992.

25. Mugge A, Forstermann U, Lichtlen PR: Platelets, endothelium-dependent responses and atherosclerosis. Ann Med 23:545, 1991.

26. Silagy CA, Neil AW: A meta-analysis of the effect of garlic on blood pressure. J Hypertension 12:463, 1994.

27. Mancia G, Grassi G, Pomidossi G, Gregorini L, Bertinieri G, Parati G, Ferrari A, Zancchetti A: Effects of blood-pressure measurement by the doctor on patient's blood pressure and heart rate. Lancet 2:695, 1983.

28. Jain RC, Vyas CR, Mahatma OP: Hypoglycaemic action of onion and garlic. Lancet 2:1491, 1973.

29. Bordia A, Bansal HC: Essential oil of garlic in prevention of atherosclerosis. Lancet 2:1491, 1973.

30. Jain RC, Vyas CR: Garlic in alloxan-induced diabetic rabbits. Am J Clin Nutr 28:684, 1975.

31. Sheela CG, Kumud K, Augusti KT: Anti-diabetic effects of onion and garlic sulfoxide acids in rats. Planta Med 61:356, 1995.

32. Chang ML, Johnson MA: Effect of garlic on carbohydrate metabolism and lipid synthesis in rats. J Nutr 110:931, 1980.

33. Nagai K, Nakagawa S, Nojima S, Mimori H: Effect of aged garlic extract on glucose tolerance test in rats. Basic Pharmacol Therapeut 3:45, 1975.

CHAPTER 6: Protection from Allergies and Environmental Pollution

1. Lau BHS, Wong DS, Slater JM: Effect of acupuncture on allergic rhinitis: clinical and laboratory evaluations. Am J Chinese Med 3:236, 1975.

2. Amonkar SV, Reeves EL: Mosquito control with active principle of garlic, *Allium sativum*. J Economic Entomol 63:4172, 1970.

3. Lau BHS: Detoxifying, radioprotective and phagocyte-enhancing effects of garlic. Int Clin Nutr Rev 9:27, 1989.

4. Cha CW: A study on the effect of garlic to the heavy metal poisoning of rat. J Korean Med Sci 2:213, 1987.

5. Wong SJ, Zhu DA: The effectiveness of S.G.P. on dental patients with mercury restorations - a pilot study. Personal Communication, 1987.

6. Nakagawa S, Yoshida S, Hirao Y, Kasuga S, Fuwa T: Cytoprotective activity of components of garlic, ginseng and ciuwjia on hepatocyte injury induced by carbon tetrachloride in vitro. Hiroshima J Med Sci 34:303, 1985.

7. Hikino H, Tohkin M, Kiso Y, Namiki T, Nishimura S, Takeyama K: Antihepatotoxic actions of *Allium sativum* bulbs. Planta Medica 3:163, 1986.

8. Kagawa K, Matsutaka H, Yamaguchi Y, Fukuhama C: Garlic extract inhibits the enhanced peroxidation and production of lipids in carbon tetrachloride-induced liver injury. Japanese J Pharmacol 42:19, 1986.

9. Nakagawa S, Masamoto K, Sumiyoshi H, Kunihiro K, Fuwa T: Effect of raw and extracted-aged garlic juice on growth of young rats and their organs after peroral administration. J Toxicol Sci 5:91, 1980.

CHAPTER 7: Cancer Prevention

1. Wigley C: Chemical carcinogenesis and precancer. In *Introduction to the Cellular and Molecular Biology of Cancer*. L.M. Franks and N. Teich, editors. p. 131, 1986.

2. Adams GE: Radiation carcinogenesis. In *Introduction to the Cellular and Molecular Biology of Cancer*. L.M. Franks and N. Teich, editors. p. 154, 1986.

3. Wyke, JA: Viruses and cancer. In *Introduction to the Cellular and Molecular Biology of Cancer*. L.M. Franks and N. Teich, editors. p. 176, 1986.

4. Lau BHS, Masek TD, Chu WT, Slater JM: Antiinflammatory reaction associated with murine L1210 leukemia. Experientia 32:1598, 1976.

5. Slater JM, Ngo E, Lau BHS: Effect of therapeutic irradiation on the immune responses. Am J Roentg 26:313, 1976.

6. Johnson JA, Lau BHS, Nutter RL, Slater JM, Winter CE: Effect of L1210 leukemia on the susceptibility of mice to *Candida albicans* infections. Infect Immun 19:146, 1978.

7. Tosk J, Lau BHS, Myers RC, Torrey R: Selenium-induced enhancement of hematoporphyrin derivative phototoxicity in murine bladder tumor cells. Biochem Biophys Res Comm 104:1086, 1986.

8. Lau BHS, Wang-Cheng RM, Tosk J: Tumor-specific T-lymphocyte cytoxicity enhanced by low dose of *C. parvum*. J Leukocyte Biol 41:407, 1987.

9. Lau BHS, Ong P, Tosk J: Macrophage chemiluminescence modulated by Chinese medicinal herbs *Astragalus membranaceus* and *Ligustrum lucidum*. Phytotherapy Res. 3:148, 1989.

10. Mei X, Wang ML, Xu HX, Pan XP, Gao CY, Han N, Fu MY: Garlic and gastric cancer. Acta Nutr Sinica 4:53, 1982.

11. You WC, Blot WJ, Chang YS, Ershow A, Yang ZT, An Q, Henderson BE, Fraumeni JF, Wang TG: Allium vegetables and reduced risk of stomach cancer. J Natl Cancer Inst 81:162, 1989.

12. Buiatti E, Palli D, Bianchi S: A case-control study of gastric cancer and diet in Italy. Int J Cancer 48:309, 1991.

13. Zheng W, Blot WJ, Shu XQ, Gao YT: Diet and other risk factors for laryngeal cancer in Shanghai, China. Am J Epidemiol 136:178, 1992.

14. Hu JF, Liu YY, Yu YK, Zhao TZ, Liu SD, Wang QQ: Diet and cancer of the colon and rectum: a case-control study in China. Int J Epidemiol 20:362, 1991.

15. Steinmetz KA, Kushi LH, Bostick RM, Folsom AR, Potter JD: Vegetables, fruits, and colon cancer in the Iowa Women's Health Study. Am J Epidemiol 139:1, 1994.

16. Steinmetz KA, Potter JD, Folsom AR: Vegetables, fruits, and lung cancer in the Iowa Women's Health Study. Cancer Res 53:536, 1993.

17. Swanson CA, Mao BL, Li JY, Lubin JH, Yao SX: Dietary determinants of lung-cancer risk: results from a case-control study in Yunnan province, China. Int J Cancer 50:876, 1992.

18. Dorant E, van den Brandt PA, Goldbohm RA: A prospective cohort study on *Allium* vegetable consumption, garlic supplement use, and the risk of lung carcinoma in the Netherlands. Cancer Res 54:6148, 1994.

19. Pan XY: Comparison of the cytotoxic effect of fresh garlic, diallyl trisulfide, 5-fluorouracil, mitomycin C and cis-DDP on two lines of gastric cancer cells. Chung-Hua Chung Liu Tsa Chih 7:103, 1985.

20. Wargovich MJ, Goldberg MT: Diallyl sulfide: a naturally occurring thioether that inhibits carcinogen-induced nuclear damage to colon epithelial cells in vivo. Mutation Res 143:127, 1985.

21. Wargovich MJ: Diallyl sulfide, a flavor component of garlic (*Allium sativum*), inhibits dimethylhydrazine-induced colon cancer. Carcinogenesis 8:487, 1987.

22. Belman S: Onion and garlic oils inhibit tumor promotion. Carcinogenesis 4:1063, 1983.

23. Sparnins VL, Mott AW, Barany G, Wattenberg LW: Effects of allyl methyl trisulfide on glutathione S-transferase activity and benzopyrene-induced neoplasia in the mouse. Nutr Cancer 8:211, 1986.

24. Liu J, Lin RI, Milner JA: Inhibition of 7,12-dimethylbenz[a]anthracene-induced mammary tumors and DNA adducts by garlic powder. Carcinogenesis 13:1847, 1992.

25. Ip C, Lisk D, Stoewsand GS: Mammary cancer prevention by regular garlic and selenium-enriched garlic. Nutr Cancer 17:279, 1992.

26. Wargovich MJ, Imada O, Stephens LC: Inhibition and post-initiation chemopreventive effects of diallyl sulfide in esophageal carcinogenesis. Cancer Lett 64:39, 1992.

27. Hussain SP, Jannu LN, Rao AR: Chemopreventive action of garlic on methylcholanthrene-induced carcinogenesis in the uterine cervix of mice. Cancer Lett 49:175, 1990.

28. Tadi PP, Teel RW, Lau BHS: Anticandidal and anticarcinogenic potentials of garlic. Int Clin Nutr Rev 10:423, 1990.

29. Tadi PP, Teel RW, Lau BHS: Organosulfur compounds of garlic modulate mutagenesis, metabolism, and DNA binding of aflatoxin B1. Nutr Cancer 15:87, 1991.

30. Beier RC: Natural pesticides and bioactive components in foods. Rev Environ Contam Toxicol 113:47, 1990.

31. Yamasaki T, Teel RW, Lau BHS: Effect of allixin, a phytoalexin produced by garlic, on mutagenesis, DNA-binding and metabolism of aflatoxin B1. Cancer Lett 59:89, 1991.

32. Amagase H, Milner JA: Impact of various sources of garlic and their constituents on 7,12- dimethylbenz[a]anthracene binding to mammary cell DNA. Carcinogenesis 14:1627, 1993.

33. Lau BHS, Woolley JL, Marsh CL, Barker GR, Koobs DH, Torrey RR: Superiority of intralesional immunotherapy with *Corynebacterium parvum* and *Allium sativum* in control of murine transitional cell carcinoma. J Urol 136:701, 1986.

34. Marsh CL, Torrey RR, Woolley JL, Barker GR, Lau BHS: Superiority of intravesical immunotherapy with *Corynebacterium parvum* and *Allium sativum* in control of murine bladder cancer. J Urol 137:359, 1987.

35. Lau BHS, Marsh CL, Barker GR, Woolley J, Torrey R: Effects of biological response modifiers on murine bladder tumor. Nat Immun Cell Growth Regul 4:260, 1985.

36. Weisberger AS, Pensky J: Tumor-inhibiting effects derived from an active principle of garlic (*Allium sativum*). Science 126:1112, 1957.

37. Weisberger AS, Pensky J: Tumor inhibition by a sulfhydryl-blocking agent related to an active principle of garlic (*Allium sativum*). Cancer Res 18:1301, 1958.

38. Sumiyoshi H, Wargovich MJ: Garlic (*Allium sativum*): a review of its relationship to cancer. Asia Pacific J. Pharmacol. 4:133, 1989.

39. Dausch JG, Nixon DW: Garlic: a review of its relationship to malignant disease. Preventive Med 19:346, 1990.

40. Dorant E, van den Brandt PA, Goldbohm RA, Hermus RJJ, Sturmans F: Garlic and its significance for the prevention of cancer in humans: a critical view. Br. J. Cancer 67:424, 1993.

41. Lau BHS, Tadi PP, Tosk JM: *Allium sativum* (garlic) and cancer prevention. Nutr Res 10:937, 1990.

42. Fujiwara M, Nakata T: Induction of tumour immunity with tumour cells treated with extract of garlic (*Allium sativum*). Nature 216:83, 1967.

43. Nakata T, Fujiwara M: Adjuvant action of garlic sugar solution in animals immunized with Ehrlich ascites tumor cells attenuated with allicin. Gann 66:417, 1975.

44. Aboul-Enein AM: Inhibition of tumor growth with possible immunity by Egyptian garlic extracts. Die Nahrung 30:161, 1986.

CHAPTER 8: Modulation of Immune Function

1. Lau BHS, Woolley JL, Marsh CL, Barker GR, Koobs DH, Torrey RR: Superiority of intralesional immunotherapy with *Corynebacterium parvum* and *Allium sativum* in control of murine transitional cell carcinoma. J Urol 136:701, 1986.

2. Fujiwara M, Nakata T: Induction of tumour immunity with tumour cells treated with extract of garlic (*Allium sativum*). Nature 216:83, 1967.

3. Nakata T, Fujiwara M: Adjuvant action of garlic sugar solution in animals immunized with Ehrlich ascites tumor cells attenuated with allicin. Gann 66:417, 1975.

4 Aboul-Enein AM: Inhibition of tumor growth with possible immunity by Egyptian garlic extracts. Die Nahrung 30:161, 1986.

5. Lau BHS: Detoxifying, radioprotective, and phagocyte-enhancing effects of garlic. Intern Clin Nutr Rev 9:27, 1989.

6. Hirao Y, Sumioka I, Nakagami S, Yamamoto M, Hatono S, Yoshida S, Fuwa T, Nakagawa S: Activation of immunoresponder cells by the protein fraction from aged garlic extract. Phytotherapy Res 1:161, 1987.

7. Lau BHS, Yamasaki T, Gridley DS: Garlic compounds modulate macrophage and T-lymphocyte functions. Mol Biotherapy 3:103, 1991.

8. Reeve VE, Bosnic M, Rozinova E, Boehm-Wilcox C: A garlic extract protects from ultraviolet B (280-320 nm) radiation-induced suppression of contact hypersensitivity. Photochem Photobiol 58:813, 1993.

9. Fisher MS, Kripke ML: Systemic alteration induced in mice by ultraviolet light irradiation and its relationship to ultraviolet carcinogenesis. Proc Natl Acad Sci USA 74:1688, 1977.

10. Fisher MS, Kripke ML: Suppressor T lymphocytes control the development of primary skin cancers in ultraviolet-irradiated mice. Science 216:1133, 1982.

11. Morioka N, Sze LL, Morton DL, Irie RF: A protein fraction from aged garlic extract enhances cytotoxicity and proliferation of human lymphocytes mediated by interleukin-2 and concanavalin A. Cancer Immunol Immunother 37:316, 1993.

12. Kandil OM, Abdullah TH, Elkadi A: Garlic and the immune system in humans: its effect on natural killer cells. Federation Proceedings 46:441, 1987.

13. Abdullah TH, Kandil O, Elakdi A, Carter J: Garlic revisited: therapeutic for the major diseases of our times? J Natl Med Asso 80:439, 1988.

14. Abdullah TH, Kirkpatric DV, Carter J: Enhancement of natural killer cell activity in AIDS with garlic. J Oncology 2:52, 1989.

15. Newberne PM, Thurman GB: Lipids and the immune system. Report and recommendations. Cancer Res. 41:3803, 1981.

16. Sanchez A, Reeser JL, Lau, BHS, Yahiku PY, Willard RE, McMillan PJ, Cho SY, Magie AR, Register UD: Role of sugars in human neutrophilic phagocytosis. Am J Clin Nutr 26:1180, 1973.

17. Ader R: *Psychoneuroimmunology*. Academic Press, 1981.

18. Ader R, Felten DL , Cohen N: *Psychoneuroimmunology*, 2nd ed. Academic Press, 1991.

19. Merritt K, Rodrigo JJ: Immune response to synthetic materials. Sensitization of patients receiving orthopaedic implants. Clin Orthop 326:71, 1996.

20. Ono Y, Nakaji S, Sugawara K, Kumae T: Effects of metals on the reactive oxygen species generating capacity of human neutrophils and on the serum opsonic activity. Nippon Eiseigaku Zasshi 49:645, 1994.

21. Daum JR, Shepherd DM, Noelle RJ: Immunotoxicology of cadmium and mercury on B-lymphocytes. I. Effects on lymphocyte function. Int J Immunopharmacol 15:383, 1993.

22. Melamed I, Kark JD, Spirer Z: Coffee and the immune system. Int J Immunopharmacol 12:129, 1990.

23. Lau BHS: How lifestyle habits affect the immune system. J Health & Healing 16:2, 1993.

24. Mutchnick MG, Lee HH: Impaired lymphocyte response to mitogen in alcoholic patients. Alcoholism Clin Exp Res 12:155, 1988.

25. Glassman AB, Bennett CE, Randall CL: Effect of ethyl alcohol on human peripheral lymphocytes. Arch Pathol Lab Med 109:540, 1985.

26. Johnson JD, Houchens DP, Kluwe WM, Craig DK, Fisher GL: Effects of mainstream and environmental tobacco smoke on the immunse system in animals and humans: a review. Critical Rev Toxicol 20:369, 1990.

CHAPTER 9: Free Radical Pathology

1. Cooper KH: *Antioxidant Revolution.* Thomas Nelson Publishers, Nashville, TN, 1994.

2. Halliwell B: The role of oxygen radicals in human disease, with particular reference to the vascular system. Haemostasis 23 Suppl 1:118, 1993.

3. Reddy KK, Bulliyya G, Chandraiah TR, Kumari KS, Reddanna P, Thyagaraju K: Serum lipids and lipid peroxidation pattern in industrial and rural workers in India. Age 14:33, 1991.

4. Martin GR, Danner DB, Holbrook NJ: Aging—causes and defenses. Annu Rev Med 44:419, 1993.

5. Gross V, Arndt H, Andus T, Palitzsch KD, Scholmerich J: Free radicals in inflammatory diseases pathophysiology and therapeutic implications. Hepatogastroenterology 41:320, 1994.

6. Halliwell B: Oxygen radicals, nitric oxide and human inflammatory joint disease. Ann Rheum Dis 54:505, 1995.

7. Hollan S: Free radicals in health and disease. Haematologia Budap 26:177, 1995.

8. Geng ZH, Rong YQ, Lau BHS: S-allyl cysteine inhibits nuclear factor kappa B activation in human T lymphocytes. Free Radical Biol Med 1996.

9 Sappey C, Leclercq P, Coudray C, Faure P, Micoud M, Favier A: Vitamin, trace element and peroxide status in HIV seropositive patients: asymptomatic patients present a severe beta-carotene deficiency. Clin Chim Acta 230:35, 1994.

10. Buhl R: Imbalance between oxidants and antioxidants in the lungs of HIV-seropositive individuals. Chem Biol Interact 91:147, 1994.

11. Sagar S, Kallo IJ, Kaul N, Ganguly NK, Sharma BK: Oxygen free radicals in essential hypertension. Mol Cell Biochem 111:103, 1992.

12. De Bruyn VH, Nuno DW, Cappelli-Bigazzi M, Dole WP, Lamping KG: Effect of acute hypertension in the coronary circulation: role of mechanical factors and oxygen radicals. J Hypertension 12:163, 1994.

13. Lau BHS: Phytochemical research at LLU. Alumni J Nov.-Dec.:8, 1995.

14. Ngo HN, Teel RW, Lau BHS: Modulation of mutagenesis, DNA binding, and metabolism of aflatoxin B1 by licorice compounds. Nutr. Res. 12:247, 1992.

15. Lau BHS, Lau EW, Yamasaki T: Edible plant extracts modulate macrophage activity and bacterial mutagenesis. Int Clin Nutr Rev 12:147, 1992.

16. Wong BYY, Lau BHS, Tadi PP, Teel RW: Chinese medicinal herbs modulate mutagenesis, DNA binding and metabolism of aflatoxin B₁. Mutation Res 279:209, 1992.

17. Wang Y, Qian JJ, Hadley HR, Lau BHS: Phytochemicals potentiate IL-2 generated LAK cell cytotoxicity against murine renal cell carcinoma. Mol Biother 4:143, 1992.

18. Li L, Lau BHS: Protection of vascular endothelial cells from hydrogen peroxide-induced oxidant injury by gypenosides, saponons of *Gynostemma pentaphyllum*. Phytotherapy Res 7:299, 1993.

19. Li L, Jiao LP, Lau BHS: Protective effect of gypenosides against oxidative stress in phagocytes, vascular endothelial cells and liver microsomes. Cancer Biotherapy 8:263, 1994.

20. Lau BHS, Li L, Yoon P: Thymic peptide protects vascular enothelial cells from hydrogen peroxide-induced oxidant injury. Life Sciences 52:1787, 1993.

21. Park CS, Li L, Lau BHS: Thymic peptide modulates glutathione redox cycle and antioxidant enzymes in macrophages. J Leukocyte Biol 55:496, 1994.

22. Yamasaki T, Li L, Lau BHS: Garlic compounds protect vascular endothelial cells from hydrogen peroxide-induced oxidant injury. Phytotherapy Res 8:408, 1994.

23. Geng ZH, Lau BHS: Aged garlic extract modulates glutathione redox cycle and superoxide dismutase activity in vascular endothelial cells. Phytotherapy Res 11:54, 1997.

CHAPTER 10: Antioxidants Whose Time Has Come

1. Li L, Zhou JH, Xing ST: Lipid peroxidation in liver and brain of adult thymectomized rats and aged rats. J Gerontol 10:345, 1990.

2. Li L, Zhou JH, Xing ST: Influence of thymus on free radical metabolism in the liver of rats. Basic Med Sci Clinic 11:32, 1991.

3. Li L, Zhou JH, Xing ST: Changes of hepatic microsomal mixed-function oxidase and plasma sex hormone levels in adult thymectomized rats and aged rats. Chinese J Appl Physiol 7:105, 1991.

4. Li L, Zhou JH, Xing ST, Lau BHS: Thymus-neuroendocrine-liver pathway. Med Hypotheses 41:470, 1993.

5. Li L, Xing ST, Zhou JH: Protective effects of gypenosides on rat hepatic lipid peroxidation and membrane fluidity damage. Chinese Pharmacol Bulletin 7:314, 1991.

6. Lau BHS, Li L, Yoon P: Thymic peptide protects vascular enothelial cells from hydrogen peroxide-induced oxidant injury. Life Sciences 52:1787, 1993.

7. Park CS, Li L, Lau BHS: Thymic peptide modulates glutathione redox cycle and antioxidant enzymes in macrophages. J Leukocyte Biol 55:496, 1994.

8. Li L, Lau BHS: Protection of vascular endothelial cells from hydrogen peroxide-induced oxidant injury by gypenosides, saponons of Gynostemma pentaphyllum. Phytotherapy Res 7:299, 1993.

9. Li L, Jiao LP, Lau BHS: Protective effect of gypenosides against oxidative stress in phagocytes, vascular endothelial cells and liver microsomes. Cancer Biotherapy 8:263, 1993.

10. Li L, Lau BHS: A simplified in vitro model of oxdant injury using vascular endothelial cells. In Vitro Cell Dev Biol 29A:531, 1993.

11. Yamasaki T, Li L, Lau BHS: Garlic compounds protect vascular endothelial cells from hydrogen peroxide-induced oxidant injury. Phytotherapy Res 8:408, 1994.

12. Geng Z, Lau, BHS: Aged garlic extract modulates glutathione redox cycle and superoxide dismutase activity in vascular endothelial cells. Phytotherapy Res 11:54, 1997.

13. Horie T, Murayama T, Mishima T, Itoh F, Minamide Y, Fuwa T, Awazu S: Protection of liver microsomal membranes from lipid peroxidation by garlic extract. Planta Med 55:506, 1989.

14. Horie T, Awazu S, Itakura Y, Fuwa T: Identified diallyl polysulfides from an aged garlic extract which protects the membranes from lipid peroxidation. Planta Med 58:468, 1992.

15. Imai J, Ide N, Nagae S, Moriguchi T, Matsuura H, Itakura Y: Antioxidant and radical scavenging effects of aged garlic extract and its constituents. Planta Med 60:417, 1994.

16. Ide N, Matsuura H, Itakura Y: Scavenging effect of aged garlic extract and its constituents on active oxygen species. Phytotherapy Res 1996.

17. Phelps S, Harris WS: Garlic supplementation and lipoprotein oxidation susceptibility. Lipids 28:475, 1993.

18. Popov I, Blumstein A, Lewin G: Antioxidant effects of aqueous garlic extract. 1st communication: direct detection using the photochemiluminescence. Arzneim Forsch 44:602, 1994.

19. Lewin G, Popov I: Antioxidant effects of aqueous garlic extract. 2nd communication: inhibition of the Cu^{2+}-initiated oxidation of low density lipoproteins. Arzneim Forsch 44:604, 1994.

20. Kojima R, Toyama Y, Ohnishi ST: Protective effects of an aged garlic extract on doxorubin-induced cardiotoxicity in the mouse. Nutr Cancer 22:163, 1994.

CHAPTER 11: Anti-aging Studies

1. Reddy KK, Bulliyya G, Chandraiah TR, Kumari KS, Reddanna P, Thyagaraju K: Serum lipids and lipid peroxidation pattern in industrial and rural workers in India. Age 14:33, 1991.

2. Martin GR, Danner DB, Holbrook NJ: Aging—causes and defenses. Annu Rev Med 44:419, 1993.

3. Lyons C, Barnhill W: We're having our say. Centenarian sisters recount their remarkable lives. AARP Bulletin 35:20, 1994.

4. Jensen B: *Garlic Healing Powers*. Bernard Jensen, Publisher, Escondido, CA, 1992.

5. Harman D: Aging: a theory based on free radical and radiation chemistry. J Gerontol 11:298, 1956.

6. Harman D: The aging process. Proc Natl Acad Sci USA 78:7124, 1981.

7. Imai J, Ide N, Nagae S, Moriguchi T, Matsuura H, Itakura Y: Antioxidant and radical scavenging effects of aged garlic extract and its constituents. Planta Med 60:417, 1994.

8. Ide N, Matsuura H, Itakura Y: Scavenging effect of aged garlic extract and its constituents on active oxygen species. Phytotherapy Res 1996.

9. Popov I, Blumstein A, Lewin G: Antioxidant effects of aqueous garlic extract. 1st communication: direct detection using the photochemiluminescence. Arzneim Forsch 44:602, 1994.

10. Lewin G, Popov I: Antioxidant effects of aqueous garlic extract. 2nd communication: inhibition of the Cu^{2+}-initiated oxidation of low density lipoproteins. Arzneim Forsch 44:604, 1994.

11. Lau BHS, Adetumbi MA, Sanchez A: *Allium sativum* (garlic) and atherosclerosis: a review. Nutr Res 3:119, 1983.

12. Lau BHS: Anticoagulant and lipid regulating effects of garlic (*Allium sativum*). In *New Protective Roles of Selected Nutrients in Human Nutrition*, Gene A. Spiller and James Scala, editors, AlanR. Liss, publisher, p. 295, 1989.

13. Lau BHS, Yamasaki T, Gridley DS: Garlic compounds modulate macrophage and T-lymphocyte functions. Mol Biotherapy 3:103, 1991.

14. Morioka N, Sze LL, Morton DL, Irie RF: A protein fraction from aged garlic extract enhances cytotoxicity and proliferation of human lymphocytes mediated by interleukin-2 and concanavalin A. Cancer Immunol Immunother 37:316, 1993.

15. Svendsen L, Rattan SIS, Clark BFC: Testing garlic for possible anti-aging effects on long-term growth characteristics, morphology and macromolecular synthesis of human fibroblasts in culture. J Ethnopharmacol 43:125, 1994.

16. Moriguchi T, Takashina K, Chu PJ, Saito H, Nishiyama N: Prolongation of life span and improved learning in the senescence accelerated mouse produced by aged garlic extract. Biol Pharm Bull 17:1589, 1994.

17. Moriguchi T, Saito H, Nishiyama N: Effect of aged garlic extract (AGE) on improvements of learning and memory performances in senescence accelerated mouse. In *The SAM Model of Senescence*, T. Takeda, editor, Elsevier Science B.V., Amsterdam, The Netherlands, p. 447, 1994.

18. Zhang YX, Saito H, Nishiyama N: Ameliorating effect of aged garlic extract (AGE) on learning behaviors in thymectomized senescence accelerated mouse (SAM). In *The SAM Model of Senescence*, T. Takeda, editor, Elsevier Science B.V., Amsterdam, The Netherlands, p. 451, 1994.

CHAPTER 12: Stress Fighter

1. Ader R: Psychoneuroimmunology. Academic Press, 1981.

2. Riley V: Psychoneuroendocrine influences on immunocompetence and neoplasia. Science 212:1100, 1981.

3. Marx JL: The immune system "Belongs in the Body." Science 227:1190, 1985.

4. Ader R, Felten DL , Cohen N: *Psychoneuroimmunology*, 2nd ed. Academic Press, 1991.

5. Takasugi N, Kotoo K, Fuwa T, Saito H: Effect of garlic on mice exposed to various stresses. Oyo Yakuri-Pharmacometrics 28:991, 1984.

6. Takasugi N, Kira K, Fuwa T: Effects of garlic extract preparation containing vitamins and ginseng-garlic preparation containing vitamin B1 on mice exposed to stresses. Oyo Yakuri-Pharmacometrics 31:967, 1986.

7. Yokoyama K, Uda N, Takasugi N, Fuwa T: Anti-stress effects of garlic extract preparation containing vitamins and ginseng-garlic preparation containing vitamin B1 in mice. Oyo Yakuri-Pharmacometrics 31:977, 1986.

8. Saxena KK, Gupta B, Kulshrestha VK, Srivastava RK, Prasad DN: Effect of garlic pretreatment on isoprenaline-induced myocardial necrosis in albino rats. Indian J Physiol Pharmac 24:233, 1980.

9. Kawashima H, Ochiai Y, Shuzenji H: Antifatigue effect of aged garlic extract in athletic club students. Clin Reports 20:8229, 1986.

10. Hiroshima University Group (G. Kajiyama): Clinical studies of Kyoleopin. Japanese J Clin Rep 16:1515, 1982.

11. Tanaka M: Clinical studies of Kyoleopin on complaints following treatment of gynecological malignancies. Japanese J New Remedies 31:1349, 1982.

12. Hasegawa Y, Kikuchi N, Kawashima Y, Ono Y, Shimizu K, Nishiyama M: Clinical effects of Kyoleopin against various complaints in the field of internal medicine. Japanese J New Remedies 32:365, 1983.

13. Kikuchi T, Nishimura Y, Tsukamoto C: Clinical effects of Leopin-5 and garlic extract on peripheral microcirculation. New Drug Clinics 43:146, 1994.

14. Okuhara T: A clinical study of garlic extract on peripheral circulation. Japanese Pharmacol Ther 22:3695, 1994.

CHAPTER 13: Candida - Friend or Foe

1. Truss CO: *The Missing Diagnosis*. P. O. Box 26508, Birmingham, AL, 1983.

2. Crook WG: *The Yeast Connection*. Professional Books, Jackson, TN, 1983.

3. Trowbridge JP, Walker M: *The Yeast Syndrome*. Bantam Books, New York, NY, 1986.

4. Crook WG: *The Yeast Connection and the Woman*. Professional Books, Jackson, TN, 1995.

5. Tadi PP, Teel RW, Lau BHS: Anticandidal and anticarcinogenic potentials of garlic. Int Clin Nutr Rev 10:423, 1990.

6. Ghannoum MA: Inhibition of Candida adhesion to buccal epithelial cells by an aqueous extract of *Allium sativum* (garlic). J Appl Bacteriol 68:163-169, 1990.

CHAPTER 14: Conclusion - The Triangle of Disease

1. Adetumbi MA, Lau BHS: *Allium sativum* (garlic) - a natural antibiotic. Med Hypotheses 12:227, 1983.

2. Tsai Y, Cole LL, Davis LE, Lockwood SJ, Simmons V, Wild GC: Antiviral properties of garlic: In vitro effects on influenza B, herpes simplex and coxsackie viruses. Planta Medica 5:460, 1985.

3. Nagai K: Experimental studies on the preventive effect of garlic extract against infection with influenza virus. Japanese J Inf Dis 47:321, 1973.

4. Guo NL, Lu DP, Woods, GL, Reed E, Zhou GZ, Zhang LB, Waldman RH: Demonstration of the anti-viral activity of garlic extract against human cytomegalovirus in vitro. Chinese Med J 106:93, 1993.

5. Lau BHS, Yamasaki T, Gridley DS: Garlic compounds modulate macrophage and T-lymphocyte functions. Mol. Biotherapy. 3:103, 1991.

6. Morioka N, Sze LL, Morton DL, Irie RF: A protein fraction from aged garlic extract enhances cytotoxicity and proliferation of human lymphocytes mediated by interleukin-2 and concanavalin A. Cancer Immunol Immunother 37:316, 1993.

7. Kandil OM, Abdullah TH, Elkadi A: Garlic and the immune system in humans: its effect on natural killer cells. Federation Proceedings 46:441, 1987.

8. Lau BHS: Detoxifying, radioprotective and phagocyte-enhancing effects of garlic. Int Clin Nutr Rev 9:27, 1989.

9. Geng ZH, Rong YQ, Lau BHS: S-allyl cysteine inhibits activation of nuclear factor kappa B in human T cells. Free Radical Biol Med 1996.

10. White EG: *Ministry of Healing*. Pacific Press, Mountain View, CA, 1905.

INDEX